I would like to dedicate my story to the gentle doctor who sowed the seed of inspiration and my beloved Lynne who nurtured it.

The Many Faces Of Love

Joan Malek

authorHOUSE®

AuthorHouse™ UK Ltd.
500 Avebury Boulevard
Central Milton Keynes, MK9 2BE
www.authorhouse.co.uk
Phone: 08001974150

First published by AuthorHouse   05/23/2011

ISBN: 978-1-4567-7075-4 (sc)
ISBN: 978-1-4567-7460-8 (dj)
ISBN: 978-1-4567-7461-5 (e)

Joan & Edna   Joan at 2

I was born on 8ᵗʰ June 1922 in a little terrace near Brighton Station, no road, just what one would now call an alley. A wonderful place for a child to be reared and to play. The house was number 4 and I had it to myself until 14ᵗʰ October 1925 when upon returning from a walk with my Father, which in itself was unusual, as he never before or after took me out by myself again, we returned and my Auntie Rose, took me upstairs to see my mother who was lying in bed and in the crook of her arm lay a tiny baby girl, Edna, as she came to be known. My immediate reaction was send it back we don't want it! My aunt put me out of the room where I promptly soiled myself in rebellion. ah my, if I only had Edna here now. But back then, when mum stood me on a chair to rock her to sleep, I used to bang the pram up and down, horrid little three year old full of sibling jealously it ran right through me. I tried often to climb back into the pram. Mum must have had a great time with me.

The next new thing to happen to me was school. When Mum took me for the first time they had to lock two desks around me so that she could get away. That left Edna queen of all she surveyed.

The following morning when requested to get up for school, I replied, I've been to school. Silly me! Thinking it was a one off, Mum said they were supposedly the best times of my life. I wondered what the rest would be like then! At school I got punished because I wouldn't stop talking and later, rapped across the knuckles with a ruler for writing poetry under the desk instead of working. I was punished for standing on a box and looking over the wall at the boys next door too, So it went on.

We went to Sunday school and I used to change my velour hat with one of the girls who wore a red beret. I asked why they wore them and was told because they were orphans. I didn't know what that was and used to go around boasting that I was an orphan, until the teacher explained that they had no Mummy or Daddy. I never changed hats back so quickly as I did then.

When I was nine years old and contracted diphtheria I was taken for swabs and then wrapped in a scarlet blanket and taken to hospital, a sanatorium. My Dad said goodbye Joanie Cocker, he thought I wasn't coming back! Mum didn't though. None of that impressed me greatly, an injection which was new to me, my parents having to look at me through a glass window, and they said for two weeks I was unconscious!

The ward I was in looked out on to the cemetery and one could see what was happening all around them in the ward. One day a little girl came in, our neighbours child, Georgina, and I said to her "you don't get out of here, you die and have to go out there". Once again I copped it, sick as I was, and had my pillow taken away from me for that. How would I have known at nine years old that we were not for the off. But eventually, very weak, I was prepared for home. Dunked right under a bath of disinfectant, all my things put in an oven before I could leave and off I went in a taxi, home.

The arches of my feet had dropped and I walked like Donald Duck, but I was made to hold a pencil in my toes until they were ok again. Understandably I was quite weak, and now at home, the boot was on the other foot. Edna had had her world established, now I was the intruder and she found she could make me weep quite easily, and did, until Mum put a stop to it. Then Mum had a really good idea, she started us at a dancing school, thinking it would help me recover, no doubt.

I had at last found my passion, at ballet I was hopeless, also at acrobats, but at tap dancing I found heaven. We had a small board at home to practice on and soon we were being enrolled in concerts. I had no singing voice but I knew my feet would salvage all of that. Once we had a show in a dance hall, maybe for a charity, I don't know, I only know that it was heaven. I was dressed in a white velvet top and knickers, a tiny cut away black skirt, top hat and a stick I had to bang on the floor in the sequence. I remember the words of the song said "come get together, let the dance floor feel your leather, let yourself go". I knew when I sang that no one would listen, just another squawking kid and they chatted on, but when I began to dance I knew I had them, they quietened down very soon and I danced a dance of joy, banging my stick on the floor, I thought I'd died and gone to heaven. The love of dancing was to last all of my life.

Then it came, the first tragedy for me. At ten years old, Andrew

Melville king of theatre came to pick children for the pantomime at the grand theatre and was I chosen. Oh the feeling of elation, footlights, I was thinking of people I would draw to me, the applause, it filled my young bloodstream. We had to be off stage by 9pm, have daily lessons and be passed by a doctor as fit. Mum took me to Lewes to be examined, bombshell, the doctor said to me Mother "this child is not going to dance, she is going home and straight to bed, not even climb stairs".

Albert (Joans Dad)

Ivy (Joans Mum)

Mum & Dads wedding

Now there I lay, on a put you up in the living room, it was rheumatism in the muscles of the heart, rheumatic fever I guess. That's how I remember it being described from the diphtheria and for four years I could do no physical exercises at school, no exertion at all. Funnily enough I didn't take it too badly, instead I used to train the neighbours kids to dance in our back yard, whether they wanted to or not. I went to school quite subdued after that, although still talking too much! But enough of schools, there were other things in our lives.

The next thing to emerge in my young life at eleven years old was puberty. I woke one morning to find the inevitable. I thought I was dying. Luckily my Auntie Frances was staying with us that weekend and explained that it was nothing to worry about. Oh yes? not my idea of a good life, bad tummy ache and the fact she said it would now occur every month, that I was a woman now and must be careful with the boys should they come into the situation. She went to my Mother who supplied the requisites and said that "there were worse things in life to come than that." Things were beginning to look better and better to me now. However, at school the next day I was proud to tell all the others that I was a woman now, whereupon I was asked to go and see the Headmistress. She was very kind, she said that I am not in any way displeased with you Joan and you are a woman now, but we don't talk about these things, only to our Mothers. I thought that won't work with mine, but she said just tell your teacher when there are times you won't want PT, or to be excused from folk dancing, for I was now able to do small things, unless I felt poorly. My heart was improving, the doctor made me run on the spot and then kept checking my heartbeat. It would be a long while until I was really fit again.

So time moved on, and I used every Sunday evening to go to

evensong with Mr and Mrs White, our neighbours and their daughter, Cynthia, who was my age and much more beautiful than me, already winning beautiful child competitions. We used to kneel and pretend to pray whilst looking through our fingers at the choirboys. One in particular, the head boy, with a beautiful head of blonde, very blonde, hair and a voice like an angel that soared into the rafters. We used to manage to be walking by St Peters just when choir practice had ended but he showed no sign of interest, much to the beautiful Cynthia's chagrin, though she never did let on.

Then one day I came out of school, now at thirteen years old and found him waiting outside on his bike, I did a double take, inwardly, but quite cool outwards. He asked if I would like to go for a walk with him the next morning, a Saturday and I gracefully accepted.

Guess where he took me, On his butchers round. He worked for Bensons, which is now a chemist that I went to for years later in life. Oh what romance, tradesman's entrances with beef and sausages, years later I was to live in one of those houses. I kept the friendship for a while, after all, the beautiful Cynthia didn't get to do the sausage round!

Years later, I went to his funeral at St Peters, hearing in my mind that beautiful voice soaring heavenwards now. Then I watched the white hearse covered with beautiful flowers drive away, standing where we had once stood waiting with beating hearts just to see him.

My fourteenth birthday suddenly loomed, belief in Santa Clause had vanished along with all its magic, birthday parties with jelly and blamanche and school friends yelling oranges and lemons, it was almost time to leave the school I had so heartedly objected to. Across the road from our school was a little sweet shop called Maitlands and the elderly shop keeper asked me if I would like to work there. My Mother was more than willing for me to do so and she obtained permission for me to leave school two months earlier than I should.

Miss Stubbs, our Headmistress, had a good talk with me and she said "remember Joan, always laugh over the desk and not behind it". This stemmed from the fact that Cynthia used to giggle behind her desk lid and as usual, I copped it. But now it seemed evident that I was approved of, at least character wise.

So I began my new life. Mrs Maitland told me that I could eat as many sweets as I liked, thinking I suppose I would soon get sick of them. However I developed a passion for buttons coconut squares and left many a hole in those boxes. The till was a little wooden affair with two bowls, one for silver and one for copper. I wonder what the computer bods of today would make of that.

The shop was a little goldmine. The boys from Sainsburys used to come in in their white counter clothes with black buttons and the Pullman boys in navy and blue. The school children never ending. I used to have to hold the Santas drink machine on the counter when they all pressed in on it.

I was quite happy there. Mum gave me a shilling to spend out of my wages and I think I earned five shillings a week. One could buy a bag of sweets on those days for a half a penny or even a farthing. I stayed there until I was fifteen and then decided that I would like to be a nanny.

I found one job with three children but Mum found out they made me do the washing and spring cleaning and I used to go home deadbeat. So we found another one in a public house called the Dover Castle and there I was very happy. I had charge of one little girl of one year old, Pat, and from then up until the war broke out I was quite content. I only had Sunday afternoons free and my idea of heaven was to take my allowance out of my wages on the way home and buy a chocolate mint bar and stroll through the level eating it. How easily we were pleased in those days.

Then the war clouds began to gather, Chamberlain went to pacify Hitler and we thought we had avoided it. But 1939 came and on 1st September the Germans went into Poland. On the 3rd we kept our pledge to them and also entered. I remember that day well. I was walking along our terrace taking Pat to see my Mother, and through an open window I heard Chamberlain's voice saying "so as from this moment we are at war with Germany". A few minutes afterwards the air raid siren went. My Mother flew out of the house to look for my Sister and I was thinking about how I would get Pat home. But I guess it was a practice run to get us prepared and for the moment, we were safe.

I remember sitting down for lunch on Sunday and my Dad said "poor, expletive poles are catching it again". I thought who are the poles and why? I was, in the not too distant future, to find out!

Meanwhile I stayed at the Dover. Pat was growing into a little girl and everyone was trying to be as normal as possible. Gradually though, the war started reshaping our lives. Black out curtains and boards were put up, wardens checked them street by street. They also held what sounded like football cheer rattles, which if used after the siren went meant the German planes were overhead. We grew to recognise their aircraft engine sound, as opposed to ours. I remember my Mother and Aunt shushing us so that they would know whether we went under the stairway or carried on.

It came in a more tangible way to the Dover Castle in the form of a little evacuee, a girl of seven called Maureen. Mrs Knowles, her Mother explained she would be my charge as well. She came from the east end of London and was far from happy about her new home. Now, I realise a child torn up by the roots from her environment and her parents must have been scared witless. The first time we sat down to Sunday lunch all together, I recall, when hers was placed in front of her she loudly announced "If you think I am (four letter word) well going to eat this, think again! At seven years old, her little body rigid, for a moment shock just stopped everything, knives and forks stopped in mid air, frozen. She was told you will be hungry then Maureen.!

Outside afterwards, Mrs Knowles said to me, Nonnie, as I was called by one there, we can't have that, Pat is just beginning to speak. From somewhere in my heart came wisdom and I said I think the best thing to do is totally ignore it, if she thinks she can shock us, she has power already. I could hear Bob and the Potman laughing in the cellar fit to burst and I guessed why, but, that was the path we took. I let her play with Pat's dolls house and pet the dog, Caeser, but she wasn't impressed and eventually she had to be sent back home to take her chances with her own people. I wonder if they made it.

Eventually I left also, Pat was at school and was growing up. I found a job with a lovely Jewish family and that changed my outlook on life altogether. I was now twenty years old. Before I took that job, I had, however reached another definite cross road in my life.

One Sunday afternoon I went with a friend from childhood and her Mother for a tea dance and while sitting there, I noticed a very handsome young airman and on his shoulder sleeve was the word "Poland". I said to Jean "that's who my Father was talking about when the war began. I'm going to excuse him" and I did. He looked a bit bewildered, probably not knowing what an excuse me dance was, but certainly not displeased. He didn't speak English, not a word, but I learnt that his name was Adam. Adam zmuda, the first man indeed in my new way of life. He managed to signal would I meet him again that evening. Now, when a handsome young man with big brown eyes and wavy hair asks you out, you go. We went to the Princes Cinema and I wore my pearls and always afterwards I called it my evening of Princes and Pearls.

I didn't want a steady relationship at that time, life was beginning to look exciting, in spite of the bombs. Some time later I was at home one evening and Mum had suggested an early night. We were just going upstairs when there was a knock at the door. Who is it, we asked, a little fearful with the black out. "It is I, Adam", came the now familiar voice. We opened the door and he said "I have come to say goodbye, I am going away from Brighton to Hucknall to train.

Some months later I had heard the tragic news that he had died in an accident on the runway before he even had a chance to fly in action. Poor beautiful young man, never to go home. I learned years later of his resting place in Newick in Nottingham. May he rest in peace the boy of my Princes and Pearls night. My first Polish friend who opened the gate for a whole new life for me.

My Sister, Edna, meanwhile was carving out a skill on the ice rink. She had a gentleman from Hurstpierpoint as her Partner, who in spite of being a very portly person, was incredibly graceful and they looked wonderful on the ice. My Mother had made Edna a lovely black velvet dress with swansdown trimmings and bought her a pair of stunning white boots, while I had to borrow mine at the rink, they were well used and weak at the ankles, giving one a very splayed look, it was an effort to stay upright whilst skating. I stayed near the safety of the barrier while Edna gracefully glided with her partner right past me. I had fun however and loved the community singing at the end, when everyone joined hands and skated together. I always managed to be on the outside and if they let go, went shooting towards the exit in the barrier. Ah, but they are happy memories.

At that time I went to work as a Nanny to my beloved Jewish family, the Resners. I was so, so happy there and was treated as one of the family and had my meals with them, except when the Rabbi was there on a Friday night. The Sabbath meal, I remember the Rabbi used to sing, he had a beautiful voice. I wanted to serve him food but because of the customs I wasn't allowed to. But Mrs Resner taught me to make him Russian tea and let me serve him with that. She used to do all the cooking herself and oh the fish, fried in matza flour and oil, lochen soup, and the biscuits! she used to make tins full of on Fridays.

I remember the first morning I was there and Mrs Resner said "come Jani", that was my name from the beginning with them, "come and have some breakfast" well, a breakfast like that should be compulsory, crisp crusty rolls with smoked salmon in them, that I had never had.

When my 21st birthday came she did all the catering for me as a present, the tables looked beautiful and in the middle was a lovely basket of flowers from my little boy, Leon. Quite a lot of poles came to my party and the Argus mentioned that the Polish air force was well represented. Some escorted us back home and suddenly I was picked up and there and then, in the terrace where I was born, I was thrown up in the air 21 times to the singing of Stolat (I think). I was wished a hundred years of life. If they had dropped me onto the nearby fence I certainly wouldn't have made it. I also received from the Resners, an opal ring surrounded by diamonds. I stayed there until eventually I went into war work.

My first job was at Allen West on admiralty work, which I quite liked. There one began to see the cruel side of the war. Someone would bring a small yellow envelope, a girl would be called into the office and not come back on to the shop floor and we all knew what that meant, a beloved husband or son missing, presumed dead. Now it was all becoming too real!

One morning, whilst eating breakfast, Lord Haw Haw, as he was known, I believe his

name was William Joyce, announced that Allen West were the next ones to be bombed and that our clock was five minutes slow. As we passed Cox's pill factory we checked the time and Allen West's clock was five minutes slow.

At about 11am the siren went and we all got up to go down the shelter but, as I looked up, I saw what looked like three milk bottles falling, turning in the air as they fell. I thought I am going to die and I couldn't move. The Manager kept saying come on Miss Long, come on. But I was rooted to the spot and the bombs missed us and hit a pub 20 minutes away from us. Many people were killed. I managed to get home only to find my Mother frantic, someone had told her it had hit Allen West, a Policeman had grabbed him and told him to stop spreading rumours! he had assured my Mother it wasn't us that got hit. But I spent weeks in bed with stress paralysis having the queens nurses, as they were called, come in everyday.

I suddenly gained my legs back in a bizarre way! A burglar tried to get into my room twice and I don't remember getting out of bed, but Mum found me in another room. " How did you get here she gasped", but I couldn't tell her. Never mind I was walking again. The next day the Police came and said they had him, a young boy, and found him sleeping in the ladies toilets. His knife was still on the inside of my window, he couldn't get it back as a friend had slammed it shut.

I changed jobs many times after that, but, after having a bad accident in a basket making factory, where we made parachute baskets, I went back for a while to my Jewish family. Leon's Mother had died at 33 and the old lady had begged me to go back to the boy, which I did. It was all very sad.

I stayed for quite a while and would take Leon out onto Regency Square green to watch the poles play basketball. One day I heard someone yelling "Bernard, come here". A lady came to collect her little boy and that is how I met Fay, who was to stay my friend for a long while.

Mrs Resner didn't mind Leon playing with him, but the parents didn't mix. However, it was when Bernard was quite ill one day, Mrs Resner sent me round with a steamed fish meal in a heat container for the boy, whose Father was supposed to be a musician, whom I'd never met. That was the way things were with Jewish people, always they helped. I used to sit in the Square weekend afternoons with Fay while the boys played and listened to an accordion being played in the Polish quarters. They were afternoons out of time, a lovely intimate soft and gentle time in the middle of a terrible war.

Soon however, much to the family's regret, I had to go back to factory work, this time where I could exercise the hand I had injured with a knife in the basket factory, trimming false teeth at Dentsply.

Working in the day, dancing every evening at the Regent or Sherrys, also the Dome and always with Polish boys. I had made a point of going to the library and swotting up on Polish history and culture and with a friend getting Polish classes started at the Brighton Technical College, so I learned the basics and the basis to be of some interest in conversation.

So the years passed and the war came to an end. My Sister, meanwhile, had met her future husband in a very funny way. She was on Sherrys balcony with a friend and they tossed a coin to see if they should go down to the dance hall. A young man by the name of Roman Skulski picked it up. My sister had met her future on the toss of a coin! Roman was in the air force, he was also the only boy my sister ever went steady with.

Yes the war was over and all the delirious celebrations. However ration books and coupons for many things stayed. We had our freedom at a price but for the poles, freedom was not their reward, Yalta took care of that. They had exchanged one dictatorship for another, their country was ravaged, Warsaw razed to the ground and now came the torture of deciding whether to return home and risk all the dangers we were hearing about or stay. Resettlement camps sprung up, papers were issued asking them to sign if they wanted repatriation or not. Countless poles decided to emigrate to Canada or Australia and many stayed here. But they could hold their heads up high, their courage was a byword, they didn't show bitterness, though they must have felt it. A proud race.

As for me, I had learned a new and beautiful culture which I would and will carry to the end of my life. I will never forget those polite, brave and generous boys who lived here and died for their country, their beloved country. My memories are with me until today, until I write these words so many years later.

Edna and Roman planned to marry and Dad had secured us for our marriages when we were born, so he had the where withal for the event. My cousin, a childhood friend and I were bridesmaids and Roman had three young air force officers as escorts for us. They arrived the day before the wedding and I was in the bath when Mum came up and said "come and see who Roman has chosen for you". I was out that bath and downstairs so fast my feet barely touched the floor. Mum's tone was about right, a tall handsome young man, Henrick was his name, blonde and blue eyed. I was beginning to warm towards Edna's day.

It was the 21st June 1946, a beautiful day. All the neighbours turned out to watch us go. I wore blue with pink cornflowers and the other two pink with blue cornflowers and Edna looked beautiful in white. Mum had had to buy coupons for all of our attire. Edna carried roses. They married in St Peters church and the reception was held at Howards by the Pavilion. It all went splendidly and then bride and groom left for their honeymoon in Ilfracombe in Devon.

Edna's Wedding

Friends kept asking me are you not jealous? Edna getting married first and three years younger than you? but I could truthfully say no to that. I didn't want to marry just for a ring on my finger it would have to be love and a lifetime together. A strange thing occurred though on that very day. A young Polish Hussar sailed from Italy to England and went to Petworth to a camp from where he came to another camp in Newhaven.

On the following bank holiday after Edna's wedding I went to old time night at the Regent with Mum, one of the bridesmaids, Jean and other friends. Suddenly I saw him, that very Hussar who had sailed here on Edna's wedding day. I turned to Jean and said "Jean excuse that tall handsome pole just passing, he's the one I'm going to marry". She will vouch for that to this day, she asked me what I had been drinking, but did it, nevertheless, I excused him, felt his arms around me and I just knew. He didn't speak a great deal of English but I invited him back to our table, his name was Ludwik and he saw me home. I remember that August night and as I walked towards my home with him, my skirts were blowing hither and thither nearly up to my waist it was so windy. We made a date to meet the following Wednesday evening and there began my story, my real story in life.

Ludwik & Joan

The next evening was a bit awkward, I had a date with another young man from a sister regiment to Ludwiks. I didn't like just to leave him standing so went to meet him to explain things, but when I told him I was sorry but that I had met someone else he was a bit piqued and asked me who it was. I just told him where Ludwik was billeted but not who and he said "oh you won't see him again they are being moved tomorrow". My hopes went down into my boots and said cheerio and sorry but decided to keep the appointment anyway.

Well, when I got there, no Ludwik! sadly, I went back home, borrowed 1s and 6 pence from my Mother and started out for the Regent. As I got to the top of the road, there he was striding towards me. The lorry had been late bringing him to Brighton. I didn't mention Bruno and we went to Sherrys, dancing. We carried on dating, getting to know each other more and more. He spoke a little English and I a little Polish and we managed fine. They had an English teacher who went to the camp at Newhaven once a week and when I asked him one day what he had learned, he said a story called "Sinsirella". I puzzled and puzzled, light dawned, it was Cinderella. One day someone phoned and said could I come up to the camp to see him as he had had a minor operation on his foot. It was a girl phoning and my hackles rose a bit, but I agreed. I think it was a number 12 bus that took me to the beginning of a very long road that led to the valley between Peacehaven and Newhaven where the camp nestled in the hollow. A group of Nissan huts that the ATS had used during the war. So it had conveniences for girls too. It was quite a walk but in loves young dream who notices. Ludwik was very happy to see me and I met all of his fellow hussars, two in particular were very friendly. One was quite a lot older than the others who was very protective, and one very young who made me a bit sad knowing how young he must have been when he left his home and family behind. That young one was to play quite a big part in my life years later, his name was Mali Kazik which translates into little Kazik. So my days spent at the camp began. It was quite a trek but in summer very nice and healthy. I used to eat with them out of a metal pan on a long handle, quite tasty things. On Sunday afternoons we would sit in the open on the steps of the huts like gypsies listening to someone playing an accordion. In the summer air it sounded lovely. One of them kept bees, which I'm scared of, another used to pick mushrooms and bring me a plate of them. He would ask "would you like grzybki janka?" Would I!

Gradually I picked up more Polish and felt quite at home among them. There was one sad day when I learned they had these wretched papers in which they were asked to sign as to whether they would go home or not. A heart searching and rending thing for anyone to do. I believe the majority stayed here or emigrated. Then one day came word that they were being moved back to Petworth, a two hour journey by us. But Ludwik and I didn't count the miles. We met until the de-mob came around and he lived in a camp (I think it was called Five Oaks) in Horsham and obtained a job in Dominics the wine store. Sometimes he spent a weekend at my home in Brighton sleeping in the bathroom which was originally my Grandpa's bedroom converted. Roman was studying for civil engineering to begin with. For some reason we didn't get along with each other very well, kind of off and on.

One day, when Ludwik and I were strolling on the fields in Horsham, he picking nuts off the trees and eating them, he said "why don't we get engaged on my nameday, 25ᵗʰ August and marry three months later, 25ᵗʰ October? Well, After I got my balance back I said Yes!

The following Sunday we were all at lunch and Ludwik said to Roman in Polish, how do I ask Joan's father if I can marry her?

Roman In English boldly said "Dad, Ludwik wants to marry Joan. Dad did a double take, he had not long had Edna's wedding. He asked when. We said in three months and he replied "can't you make Christmas a double celebration", but no we wanted 25th October. While stacking dishes I heard my Dad in the kitchen say to Mum, Ive, is there any reason for the rush. We had him worried so I called out "No there is not we just want that date". So it was all stations go, we were on. Looking back now I think I got the two reasons for me visiting him mixed up in Newhaven. He didn't have enough money left to take me out so a reason was found for me to go to Petworth, the foot problem. But really, now, what does it count or matter for, we were always together and now we were going to be married.

So Mum was once again buying coupons for the bridal dresses. Mine was a white silky material with embossed lily's of the valley, veils were unobtainable so mine had to be a tulle with a headband of white feathers to keep it in place. It was still difficult as it was so light a breath of wind made it precarious, but the effect was quite as I would want. I carried white chrysanthemums and the girls, Jean, Silvia and my cousin Pat were blue with bronze chrysanthemums. Mum always managed these things, we found a dressmaker in Cleveland Road, I can't recall her name, I just remember standing on the table while she pinned my skirt to the right length.

It was a lovely day but quite fresh when we were married in St Josephs church, Elm Grove. Father Munn married us, I couldn't have a nuptial mass as I was still taking instructions which I was quite enjoying with Father Walsh at St Mary Magdalenes. I was quite nervous and my friend said I looked as if I was going to my doom, so serious I was. I wished afterwards that I would have walked down the aisle again and enjoyed it more. But everything went well, the reception was held in my old school hall and my headmistress greeted us and wished us well, also with instructions not to put glasses on her piano. Still the same dear lady who had chastised me so often as a child. We danced and everyone seemed to enjoy themselves. Roman kept feeding the guests so they wouldn't get drunk and ended up getting tipsy himself, he forget to eat, he was so busy. Edna walked him on to the seafront to get him to clear his head. Then the band played now is the hour and we left to change to leave for our weekend honeymoon, we couldn't afford more. But we did go up on the Brighton Belle and we were supposed to have a night of luxury at the Eaton hotel but they had mis-booked us and we had to go to a boarding house they had found, where the landlady spotted confetti on the bathroom floor and came up with some spicy remarks. However, we were alone together at last. It was a beautiful thing to snuggle down together on a chilly night and forget the world outside.

Ludwik & Joan

Ludwik & Joan's Wedding Day

Next day we spent at Regents Park Zoo. How exotic can one get but it was enjoyable and then home to the Mundane. But we had lunch at Lyons Corner House and listened to the music and I wore my little home made engagement ring, two hearts joined together made out of a piece of air craft metal. To me it was worth all the diamonds in the world, I still have it. Then back home to Mums were we all lived together. Roman and Edna also hadn't found anywhere. It was difficult in those days, I had various jobs, for Ludwik, it was more difficult not being a British subject, but as a skilled moulder, Ludwik went to Lewes and applied at the foundry for a job. He held all the necessary qualifications and indeed was a qualified man at his trade. He was told quite kindly, I should love to take you on but I would have a strike on my hands taking on a foreigner. Great, fit to fight by their side but not to work, so much for Mr Churchill's promise of that aspect.

I went to the labour exchange and enquired of a rather dour young man what work my husband was allowed to do. Oh, he replied airily, anything an Englishman won't do. I replied quite coolly "well he does want an honest job and certainly he won't accept charity". I went round to all the back doors of the hotels, who kept offering me a job, only to explain it was for my husband! The Manager at the Metropole, a Mr Hicks was very kind and said send him along to see me love. So Ludwik began his working life in England washing dishes in the kitchen, a veritable reward for fighting alongside us and losing his country. But it was an honest job, very low wages but we were happy just to be together.

My only worry now was the fact that after two months there was still no sign of a baby, and I did want a family.

But, before I sorted that one out I kept hearing on the radio an appeal for moulders and my blood was running hot over that. Eventually I said to my Father , blow this I am going to see Mr Teeling our MP at that time, which I did. He asked if I wanted him to fight the Unions, my reply was yes please, just as he helped you fight for your freedom. Somewhat chastened he gave me the address to write to him at the house which I promptly went home and did. I scorched the paper with all the feelings I felt at that moment. The next morning Mr Teeling was at mass at St Mary Magdalene's and as we came out he touched my hand and said don't forget, write to me. I replied curtly its in the post. Oh, he said you don't let the grass grow under your feet young lady. I thought you haven't seen the half of what I will do for my man yet. Within a week I must say I received a very polite and kind letter from Major Beamish, MP for Lewes apologising for our difficulties and stating a plan he had thought out. Every foundry had an annexe in Portslade, not in the Union, and he wrote "if your husband is prepared to start as a labourer, we will place him there and progress as we go along." Ludwik was to give a weeks notice at the Metropole and then begin in the annexe. The Manager was sorry to let him go, he then offered him the job of Commissionaire at the front door, but of course that was out of the question. He had to report his new job at the labour exchange, but I was given permission to do that for him. I made a point of going to the same dour young man. "Who told him he could do this?" he almost barked at me! quietly I replied "the Ministry of Labour actually" after a quick change of mood I was very politely taken to a Mr Slater the Manager and all was fait accompli!

So Ludwik began in the small foundry. One day a very untidy looking man came in and asked who is the Pole here?" Ludwik stood up and said "me, have you a problem?". He just said "could you step outside a moment please" it was Mr Every himself, the boss! He said "calm yourself, I only wanted to ask if you could pass on some tips as to how the foundries' work over there and if there are any ways we can improve some things?" Ludwik knew how to make non porous castings, but, didn't mention it, he kept that for much later.

Soon he was asked to join the Union and go to Lewes, which he refused unless someone came with signed papers, he didn't want another insult or knock back. So it was and he worked in Lewes for ten years, meeting Marcel and Tony who would figure largely in his life then and destiny later in life.

In the meantime, one February in 1951 I think it was, or maybe 1952, Mum and Ludwik had been sharing a football coupon every week and this particular day she was unwell, a kidney chill. Dad was checking the coupon and suddenly said "Ive, weve done it, 7 draws and 1 away, 2nd divi! Mum told him to stop playing the fool she didn't feel good, he said "alright then, check for yourself." Well! Mum got better so quickly it was hard to believe.

On the following Wednesday Ludwik said he would buy the paper on the way to work and if it wasn't much would go straight on. Dad couldn't wait though and went to the papershop himself. Well, he said to me, "I don't know what your old man calls a lot! but we had £700.00 each "(quite a little bit in those days) so whoopee I thought, that (or some of it) means a deposit on a house, never mind we didn't have furniture or carpets, curtains will do and the small bits we have. So after a few days we went to the estate agents.

We had been happy living with my parents with the exception of my losing our first baby. We went to the Regent Cinema to see a James Bond film, 007, and right at a critical moment someone behind me screamed and went into an epileptic fit. I felt the baby kick and on the way home thought I couldn't stop passing water, but Mum realised I had gone into labour and the doctor called an ambulance to take me to hospital. After 24 hours I had a little son, but he was stillborn. It was Christmas time and a very very sad time for us, but one has to get over these things and I was determined to try again. I had been right in the first place about something being wrong and my gynaecologist had examined me under the anaesthetic and righted a small fault and now here I was back where I started. No more films for me when I had another pregnancy. Funny enough the sister in the hospital told me the chap who had the fit was in the ward above me, how strange is fate, he never got to know about me. How hazardous our lives can be!

But now we had a new start and almost walked into another mishap, I was pregnant again, as we prepared to look for our house. The above mishap almost occurred because we gave a cheque for £250.00 as a deposit to an Agent without consulting our Solicitor and he contacted us and advised us to ask for our money back as the owner of the house we wanted wouldn't deal with this particular Agent. When we asked for it he hesitated and seemed to be playing for time, I was by this time, panicking. But Mum sat on his home doorstep and refused to budge without the cheque. Eventually a hand came round the door and handed it to her. Of course the cheque bounced, didn't it. Well he was threatened at that point with action and he said he would present the money the next day by 3pm. The Bank in those days closed at that time. The Manager told us he would phone us as soon as he had the cheque and cleared it. At two minutes to three he phoned and said he has just walked in and its now all ok. By then I was nearly passing out! but we had learned a good lesson and were never that green again. A friend told us he had borrowed from all and sundry to pay the money from £5.00

upwards and on the Friday after he went bankrupt, so by the skin of our teeth our dream was saved.

The house we chose was in Coldean Lane opposite the woods leading to Stanmer Park, three bedrooms, one of which would make a perfect nursery if my child would be safely born in time.

One afternoon, Ludwik, my parents and I went out to measure up for curtains and later in the day there was a ring at the bell. I opened the door and a very petite auburn haired lady stood there with a large tray upon which was a full English tea for four. "I thought you might be glad of this" she said "just leave the tray on my step when you go." Well, I thought as I thanked her, this bodes well for neighbours.

I couldn't wait to move in and in November we did, what joy to have a place of our own. We had so little furniture that on Sunday afternoons we moved it into the lounge, lit a roaring fire and revelled in eating our tea in front of it. The lady on the other side asked me in one afternoon for a cup of tea and she sort of skirted around asking me outright how come we could afford to be there. So I said it! "Bess, if we are going to be friends lets start off right. If you want to know how a Pole and probably the first foreigner to live up here can afford to, we won the football." There I said, "now if anyone asks you can tell them." She blushed, but accepted openness between us and from then on we were firm friends. She had four children from two years old up to 13, all very well behaved and always willing to help me. Eveline the youngest used to run home when Ludwik came home from work, perhaps his accent or foundry clothes were not usual up there! Then one day when Ludwik was painting the outside of the house she went to her Mother and said "him next door is up the ladder painting" and Bess said " well why don't you go and watch him." So the little mite sat on the steps and became friends. Bess, when my time was approaching, gave Ludwik her clothes prop and said if Joan needs a telephone don't put this through the bedroom window but call me with it if you need me.

One night we did, a little too soon, I went to hospital and my second son was born, but he didn't live, another very empty, sad time for us. Through that time Freda and Jack from the other side of us came into our life. Freda came bringing cakes or something, I don't recall, but she said "I heard you have lost your baby and thought I would come round." So we now had friends on both sides, life went on.

Bessie's husband, Bill and Ludwik built garages with a mutual walk, our garden flourished and life was quite happy.

Then one day we had the sad news that Ludwik's Father had died, now he would never see him again and a few months later his Brother, Peter, wrote to say he would like to come to England and visit us. So after all the necessary papers had been issued we went up to Liverpool Street Station to meet him. He stayed for just a week but during that time our life was to change because of what transpired. Ludwik took his Brother to see the foundry and he was not very impressed and asked him why he hadn't started up his own business. That sowed the seed for big changes, Ludwik and Tony, a compatriot that worked with him decided to do just that. Another Pole we knew who had a small plastics factory in Hove said to Ludwig "you want to start? Well start here, dig a little hole, make your furnace and begin". Now that sounds a bit Alice in Wonderland but that's just what they did on Boxing day. I think it was 1957 they made their furnace and they had already put out feelers for work and they began. Slowly they built their little foundry and began making a name for themselves in Crawley and Burgess Hill etc. Large cars would pull in there and although they were a bit embarrassed about the premises and crude furnace, one customer said "son, if this is the kind of work you can produce here, what will it be like when you have your own foundry".

Not long after that, Mike for some reason wanted the space they were in and asked them to leave. They were devastated, but as luck would have it the metal man called in the next day and he said "what's wrong mate you look a bit down in the mouth". When he heard why, he said "I've got just the place for you boy, someone in Hurstpierpoint wants to sell the lease of his foundry. Why don't you go and see him". And that's how it happened, they went to see Mr Cootes, talked seriously and spoke to my Father's Solicitor. They obtained a loan and there a dream was realised for the first time.

They moved like gypsies in an old van, equipment kept falling off, it must have been like a funny film but Ludwik was in heaven. Surprisingly the Bank allowed them an overdraft and the business gradually grew, word spread about their non porous castings and soon they had to take on help. Then other great changes began to take place, Mum and Dad decided to move into the house Grandma had left him and Dad suggested we sell our house for more capital and move into their basement. I was sad to leave my lovely home but that's just what we did, things moved on and on. Then Dad decided to move, sold the house and we moved into Stanford Avenue into one of the houses where as a thirteen year old, Jimmy Pumphrey the choir boy and butcher boy and I had delivered sausages. How strange the wheels of fate turn, that which we could never have dreamed of or expected.

Mum and Dad had been talking about Ludwik and I owning our own house again and maybe for them to live with us, they were getting older and thought we should be on our own ground just in case. Further down the Avenue there was a beautiful double fronted corner house and Mum had marked it off in the Argus for us to see, it was lying on the table when we came home from work. So that evening we made arrangements to go down and view it. We were sad as we prepared to leave my Father's house some of it's history was so happy.

We made a new circle of Polish friends in an interesting and prophetic way. Ludwik had been visiting factories in Burgess Hill, seeking orders and at one called Cleo Engineering, on meeting the Manager, learned from him that managing one of the departments there was, as the Manager put it, one of Ludwik's co-patriots. Ludwik was taken to meet him and so in this fashion, Alex Bennett (change of surname) entered our life.

Peter had been to visit us and we were hoping to plan a holiday and see him in Poland.

One day Ludwik invited Alex home to convince me it was now safe to go to Poland, for I was afraid for Ludwik after the stories I had heard. So I prepared tea and Alex duly arrived. A very elegant personable young man who reassured me on the subject of our visit. There was something about this man that made one feel safer. We chatted for a while and I kept getting drawn back to his face, I don't know why but I felt he was observing me. However, after a very pleasant afternoon we said our goodbyes and I didn't think about it after that, except to think that we will visit Poland, which we did and it was everything I had ever imagined. The feel, the smell of the people, Mickiewicz personified. The first little village we went through, a woman and a little boy were shooing geese across the road, a long straight road that ran for miles through forests. At Opole we picked up a young student to take him on to the station, but he offered to guide us all the way to Krakow. He then left us and we quite simply could not find our way to Peter's. It was midnight already so we went to Ludwik's Stepmothers, his own Mother had died when he was seven years old.

Oh, what a welcome we received. In no time, food was on the table and tea at 2am in the morning. At 3am in bed at last, I said "what's that funny light?" dawn Ludwik replied "go to sleep now". It was as Alex said quite safe although we had to be careful we didn't discuss politics with windows open, things like that and seeing more guns on policemen than I had ever seen in my life. Then we went to Peter's and the children had thought heaven had come in the form of toys and sweets, they had none, none at all. Matthew slept with his little toy car and it was never out of his reach. On the whole our holiday was joyous and wonderful. In Zakopane we went up Gerwont the mountain and it was so beautiful, the first mountain I had ever seen. We stood with one foot in Poland and one in Czechoslovakia in the snow. We didn't dare venture further over. One could hear the sound of the little bells around the sheeps necks and the shepherd would greet us with "niech pochwalony jezus chrystas" and we would answer na wieki wiekow amen", roughly translated let Christ be praised and the answer we gave forever and ever amen. I remember I stood there looking out at all the beauty and whispered "thank you Adam Zmuda but for you I might never have found this and all I have in my life now". Strange how points of time come together in our life. I could write forever in Poland but I must now take us back to England and carry on with our life there. We visited once more in 1965 and then, well that is yet to come.

Alex in the meantime, had invited us to his bungalow in

Burgess Hill where we met his daughter and also some of his friends who were going to come very close to us also in friendship. Olga and Zbyszek who were also starting up their own business making jewellery and made quite a success of it, gaining a contract with Samuels a well known jewellery firm. Also Wanda whom I grew close to and would be a good friend to me in the future. So our life was expending socially, we often all met up at Polish dances and functions and I became aware that Alex was somewhat attracted to me and I suppose all women are pleased of attention of that kind. Anyway now came the big change, we went down to view the house Mum had marked out for us and we both fell in love with it. It was big enough for all of us and also Mrs File, The lady who had had the top floor of Dad's house. So we contacted the Agent a Mr Winchester who asked us if we had a Solicitor and as we didn't, said he knew an excellent one called Mr George Cole and he did prove to be excellent, and was soon to be of immeasurable help to me. Then he wrote to us and told us that someone had put in a higher offer but the lady of the house said that if Ludwik had a gentleman's agreement with her and gave her his word we could have it at the original price, so Ludwik did just that and the sale proceeded. Then came the day when we moved in, we had our builder, Mr Adams and his workforce take down the wall between the dining room and lounge and make the electric wiring safe etc. We had plans to go to Poland in a few weeks and so Ludwik suggested we go and make our Wills so that Mum and Dad would be alright if we had an accident on the road. We made an appointment for the following Wednesday. I had been in Crawley to a stone mason and designed a fire place in Yorkshire stone. Also we had been to Worthing to pick the lighting we wanted, chandeliers for the lounge and side lights. The lounge was to be Swedish style, I had picked the wall paper for each end of the now huge room and ordered more carpet to match the one there. I had also been to the dressmaker and was having new clothes made for our trip. Ludwik had said we had now reached a point whereby I could have the things I wanted after ten years hard work.

On the Wednesday we went to Mr Coles and made our Wills and work was going ahead. The fireplace arrived and it took 6 men to bring it in. When it was in on that very Wednesday I suddenly felt frightened. I put my hand on the fireplace and I thought, I have too much god, take something away.... Oh god soon that was to happen, very soon.

On the Saturday of that week, Ludwik and Tony had a meeting at a restaurant in Bognor, The Thieves Kitchen, with somebody important from Birmingham. I can't remember if it was from Becca or Raliegh but it could have meant an excellent contract. On that day, Marcel who worked with them in the foundry decided he would go in to earn an extra penny as he put it. So they decided to drop him off, taking a different route to the one they would have.

When Tony drew up early on Saturday I suggested he come in and have a look around but Ludwik was anxious to be off. "When we come back" he said. I watched from the window as he went to say hello to Marcel in the front seat, then lit up a cigarette and climbed into the back, Ludwik's car was being overhauled before our trip to Poland. I waved goodbye and watched as the car slowly crossed over to the left and drove down the Avenue. I then went up to my parents' bedroom and for some reason I said "Ludwik really likes to drive himself, but I expect Tony is okay". I dressed and went to work as usual and during the morning there was a slight altercation between a customer and one of my staff, which I smoothed out and forgot.

After lunch I was checking out the Lego stand for reordering when the Manager came up and asked me if I could spare a moment to come up to the office, Mr Trangmar, a very diplomatic man. I thought the other staff were watching me rather funny and then thought oh that blooming do this morning, I suppose my last normal thoughts, maybe forever. Mr Trangma said a lady wants to speak to you and the office staff quietly left. Still as yet I was okay, then I turned and my Mother was crawling up the stairs, behind her a Policewoman. Straight away I knew, "Ludwik "I said, and it was as if a shutter came down behind me. Mum was shaking like a leaf! hardly able to stand. "Oh god Joan," she said, "all three." I was numb and dumb, the Policewoman said to the Manager, "make her cry, now, or she will pay all her life." Give her a brandy or something". But I couldn't feel anything, I just said, of all things, "it took ten years to build that foundry." They took me home where my poor Dad was standing, ashen white, I was afraid for his heart. Then the policewomen said "you will have to come down to the station to make a statement". I asked "how can I, I wasn't there". But we went and I was asked where were they going because the car was facing back to Brighton and they thought Ludwik was driving as his hands were on the wheel. I can only think now that he tried to save them. I learned it was a policeman running away from Slough in a stolen police car, he had been stealing for four years. In the Argus they called him the Magpie Policeman. But why would I care about that now, my beloved Ludwik would never be coming home that day to eat the lunch my Mother was just taking out of the oven for him, when the Police came. The Policewomen had cleared the kitchen up for my Mum so we went back home again and people were already gathering there. But we had to go and identify them. so they would know which husband to take us to. A Polish Priest was called to accompany me to the mortuary hospital. When I got there,

Tony's wife, Eileen, and Marcels wife Laurie, were already there crying. I couldn't, I went in with Father Pucharski who came from Ludwik's town, Krakow. I just knelt and told him I loved him and always would. Then we went home. My poor parents had cleared spaces among the building of the work that was going on and got our chairs out to make it civilised for me. I went to the phone and rang Alex, Lala his daughter answered, she went very quiet and then said I will go and fetch my Father, who was transplanting plants in his garden. Oh my god, he said, shall I come over? No, I replied, but please go to Worthing and tell Olga and Zbyszek, we were supposed to go to them tomorrow, she is cooking a Polish lunch. She had rung earlier in the week to ask what he would like. Alright, Alex said, I'll come around later. The next hours were a busy blur, word had spread and folk were coming. Then Alex and Lala came and as she sat there, poor young girl, tears were running silently down her cheeks. I thought what precious tears for me and I was very grateful.

Dr Lindeck had been my doctor from childhood and wanted to leave some pills for me, but I said I would manage. Good girl he said but I must insist on sleeping tablets for you and your Mother. Mum slept with me that night and my poor Father slept alone. He had loved Ludwik so much it probably felt like the end of our world to him. In a way it was, the world as we knew it together. The Doctor had left a number for my Mother to ring if things changed for me, in any way, just call, he said. Good advice! The morning came and I dressed and then I can't remember how but I stood at the top of the stairs and called Mum. They say that I howled like an animal in pain. My Mother flew to the phone and it seemed in no time at all Dr Shaw had arrived. I was lying on my bed he had given me a equimil, a magic pill for me. I talked and talked while Dr Shaw held my hand, I said I loved him so much Doctor, not the mushy kind, I really loved him. He let me keep talking and I fell asleep. Mum said when he left he was crying.

The days passed like lead, the workmen were asked to come back, one said he couldn't, he couldn't take my grief on board. The Priest came and we arranged the funeral, we had had to wait for a little, while formalities were proceeded with. Marcel's Brother wanted them to be buried together but I didn't want that to happen and I was right it would have led to a lot of conflict. So the funerals were all separate, Ludwik's was held in St Josephs where we were married. His Brother, Peter, had come from Poland but he was not as comforting as I expected. Things later got quite unpleasant but sufficient unto the day.

The weather that day was truly beautiful, the sky an Italian blue, the sun warm. As I left the house, Alex arrived and gave his little bow of greeting, I was so glad to see him, he had thought he maybe couldn't come. I asked him to take photos for the family in Poland, which he did of the ceremony from beginning to end. The hearse arrived, so many beautiful flowers, some in the form of the Polish flag with an eagle on it. When we arrived at the church two Priests awaited us. My beloved Father Wojtus and Father Pucharski, who was from Ludwik's town. They led us down the aisle with the customary prayers in Polish.

The service was beautiful and we came out, again into the beautiful sunshine, July, and I thought of the song, it's so hard to die when all the birds are singing in the sky. But mostly I was numb. There were so many people gathered in the cemetery, the spot where we laid him, overlooked right over the town and it was right opposite a little chapel not used anymore, but nice to see.

Then it was back home, I was carrying in my mind the day I had walked down that very aisle as a bride, memories at that time though would avail me nothing. My house was full, Ludwik's regiment had come, folk I didn't know, I was only worried as to if there would be enough food and drink and I didn't want to let Ludwik down on this, his day. But Mike put a stop to it and said my Mother should take me to rest, but ,I didn't want to and couldn't anyway. Then it was all over, the house empty, but for me, my Parents and my Aunt. Alex had promised to call the moment he got back from Poland and I knew he would.

Dad, Auntie, Mum and I went back up to the cemetery in the afternoon and we had laid fir tree branches on the grave, as is custom in Poland until the stone is placed. Also the red and white ribbons that the family had worked their names on. An old gardener came over and said "Pole was he? I knew a lot of them in Italy. I'll watch it for you and keep the ribbons there, if there's a wind I'll put it all right again." On the hilltop there would be wind, natures song for him.

Dad took me up there regularly until, gradually, I no longer needed to, soon I would place his stone. I had ordered Italian marble with a cross, a Polish eagle would be carved complete with crown under which would be his photo. It would be inscribed with the words "Here in the land of his adoption sleeps Ludwik Kostecki, Son of Poland", followed by who he was leaving and at the bottom, under thy protection. I could do no more for him until the blessing of the stone which would come much later. So was accomplished all I could do for my man from the day I fought for his right to work, through the years of building his dream, the foundry, until now where he would rest beneath his eagle buried with the epaulettes from his army uniform and a rosary from St Patrick's Cathedral in New York which my Mother's friend had sent. Now had to begin a new era, how oh how could I do it.

Ludwiks Grave

As it happened, with the help of many people.

First Alex was forever near and Mrs Howell, my Solicitors Secretary said to me one day in the King and Queen where she had persuaded me to go, she said "Joan, I'm not satisfied with how your Doctor is handling this. If I speak to my Doctor, Dr Myers and if he agrees, will you come to see him. I was too dazed to do anything but acquiesce.

The Doctor, kind man that he was, agreed and an appointment was made and so it was that I walked through the doors of the Preston Park Surgery and was to stay. It became my womb in the difficult years that followed. When I disrobed for examination, knowing at six stone I looked like a victim of Belsen, Dr Myers simply said "poor old thing" and I knew I was going to like and trust him. I was prepared to listen and try, god bless Mrs Howell. Meanwhile Alex was coming three times a week and taking me to his home, Wednesday, Saturday and Sunday, my days of comfort and peace. He tried to get me to eat but I wasn't ready yet, all I had was a raw egg beaten in milk everyday, my clothes hung on me. I never did know what happened to the ones that were being made for our trip to Poland, that time was blasted into space. His Brother had a letter sent from the Polish Embassy trying to wind up Ludwik's estate, that's the law over there apparently, but Mr Coles wrote and told them, Ludwik was a British subject and British law would take care of that. But I'm a little ahead of myself, before that, tragedy had hit us again, after only a few months had elapsed. In the meantime Alex and I had grown closer, I asked him to take me to see Dr Zhivago and although he had seen enough of the real thing, he took me. He held my hand and caressed just my thumb, it's surprising just how stirring that can be. But I was spellbound by the film, the scenery, the powerful Pasternak coming to life on the screen. I had already seen it with Ludwik and had needed to go back to it. The music will live with me forever, the field of daffodils, the icehouse in the moonlight, the howling of the wolves, I was there. After the cinema we went for a coffee and we drove home. On the way up the Avenue, Alex stopped the car by the side and we kissed for the very first time, it would not be the last, for quite a while anyway. It was comforting and affectionate and warm.

The next time we were alone in the bungalow and sitting side by side on the couch, Alex whispered one word, yes? quite softly a question. I acquiesced by gently taking my clothes off and we lay by the fire, but things didn't go quite to plan and I had to reassure him that "these things happen". I dressed and put my arms around him promising that soon things would transpire as we wished. Maybe he felt a little guilty, though, I didn't.

Sure enough the next time he drove me home after persuading me to eat, a little crisp rolls and smoked salmon, we retired without words to the bedroom. The lamp in the room was a beautiful ship with sails, as I remember. Alex sat close to me and gradually we approached what had long waited in the wings, he admired my black lingerie and gently we lay down side by side and he came to me, as he entered my body, that had been waiting for this moment without me fully realising, he whispered "dream come true" and said "this is all love". And love it was, so wonderful it defies description, while the little lamp lit ship sailed on, casting shadows on the ceiling.

We drove home at midnight, which did not please my Mother, she hated me being with Alex and did her best to part us, which was quite traumatic for me, being caught between heaven and hell.

The weeks went by, Christmas Eve with him and his newly wedded daughter Lala and her husband, He came to fetch me and Lala whispered as I went through the door, look happy about the tree, Dad's been up all night dressing it. It was a dream, all sort of mystical with a kind of white and silver cobwebby mist hanging all over it. Very very beautiful and it was all for me. I asked "may I have one of the sweets off it?" you can said Alex, but it will be musty they've been in the loft for years. We had supper together and then at 10pm we all drove into Brighton to St Josephs for mass and afterwards home again, alone as the young pair wanted their time together and come to that so did we! Sweet was our love making but I had tears on my cheeks, my feelings quite mixed I suppose and it was the first Christmas after my beloved Ludwik's terrible ending. But Alex understood, don't cry he said, I'm here and kissed them away.

Alex

Then I went home to spend a very sad Christmas with my poor grieving parents and my Aunt. So it passed, the first one after the tragedy that wrecked our way of life. I spent New Years Eve at Alex's he gave a party. Olga and Zbyszek came and I think Wanda and some neighbours also Lala and some of her friends. So we had to begin a New Year. Things got a little strained at home, Mum was getting very nasty towards Alex, he was still married although he hadn't lived with his Wife for a long time. He then told me he was getting a divorce and I said not for my sake Alex we can never marry you know that, my faith would not allow it. Although we had sinned in the eyes of the church, to me, it felt like pure love.

So we went towards Easter before which on February the 10th I had had to leave my job at Beals as toy buyer and as I no longer felt responsible enough to do it, my grief was still very real in spite of being with Alex. On that particular day Alex told me that he went every year on that evening to a do at the George, I think in Burgess Hill. He said he would meet me from work and if I asked him not to go, he wouldn't, he would stay with me, but, I said you must go Alex, I want you to have some life. I knew we had no future, much as that hurt deep and deeper. So he met me and off he went to his friends. That moment was to change our future and our lives forever. I must correct a fact, my Father had been aware of Peter's attempt to take everything from me, he said he had expected it by his behaviour. So it occurred long before the second approaching tragedy. At this moment, sometimes the facts get a little out of line but as I have written Alex's night out changed the points on the line again, such is fate. I think still that I made the right decision, we couldn't follow that path forever, beautiful as it had been with Alex bringing me daffodils and saying you get one more for every year, it would be 43 by now. But I digress.

The next day when Alex picked me up he was full of his night with his friends taking great pains to say they had a dance, where they got the chance to kiss some beautiful young ladies, great fun, he said. I don't know if that was meant to provoke some envy but he looked disappointed when I quietly replied I was pleased he had enjoyed himself.

That evening was the first of the cooling and emotional ones that were to come. Easter was approaching and we had talked about going to Portugal together, but now I didn't want to and out of the blue Alex said he was going away for Easter anyway. It made me sad but the scene was set, he said if you feel lonely go over to visit Lala she will be pleased to see you and I will tell Alan to drive you home afterwards. Just before Easter I went up to my hairdressers. My beloved friend John, he had done hairdressing for my whole family including Ludwik. I told him I was sad ,and why, he said ring him and ask him to come tonight before he goes. So I did and I said go to the house, don't mind Mum I won't be long. He agreed. However he wasn't there, I felt so hurt and afterwards I discovered why. The next day, Good Friday, I went over to Lala's and asked her if she knew why he hadn't come. You tell me she said, he went and came back here in a right old temper. He said, "women, I'll never understand them and I'll die young, a prophecy. I asked Lala to take me to the bungalow, I just wanted to be there. When we got there she said there is something funny Janka, Dad never leaves anything untidy when he goes away, but his discarded clothes were thrown on the bed, an empty glass on the draining board, he had indeed gone off in a strop. I looked around, my photo was still on the bedside table, the slippers and dainty negligee he had given me lying in their usual place. But then Lala had told me that he had gone to relations of a women he had met on his night out. Isabella, ten years younger than me and to top it all, the widow of Wanda's Brother. I could imagine what she would think about that! However, I sadly went back home, why would I care. Easter passed, I felt so low I rang Laurie, Marcel's widow and said Laurie if I pay, will you go away for a few days with me. She agreed, and said that she would ring her Sister in Frome, which she did and it was agreed that we would go with Laurie's two younger children for a week. We set off with the children in the back seat singing Edelweiss. It was the saddest, or almost, week we ever had. Her Sister seemed to resent me, I was the bosses Wife and Laurie was a widow because of me and her life was ruined. Oh god I thought, doesn't she know they were friends. However the week soon passed and I was so glad to go home, even though when we got there Mum and Dad were sitting alone in that big empty house listening to music. The emptiness closed around me, I wanted Ludwik, I needed Alex and his protecting arms which were probably around another woman right now. My own fault but I knew I had done right. To make matters worse the letter I had sent to him from Frome was unopened and sent back.

I can't really remember a lot of what happened in the weeks to follow. I know I packed his gifts up neatly and asked him to come and see me, which he did and the look on his face when I handed him his presents and letters. He was shocked but he just took them and left. My Dad said that was really a bit much Joan. However things dragged on until one day, May 22nd 1968 I said I'm going over to finish this for once and for all. Dad didn't want that but I knew it would be better for us all. Well, did I get a shock when I got to the bungalow no one was apparently at home. I looked through the window of the garage and to my amazement there was a racing car of some kind, a cute little number. I knew then I was in for trauma, I walked down to Lalas and she said "Dad has just called in for some butter and gone back home". He opened the door and said we have a visitor, took me into his, our bedroom and there in the bed lay Isabella. We had a car crash and Iza couldn't go home. I quietly said "I'm sorry to hear that" and turned to go. Alex and I looked at each other one more time and he closed the door behind me and I walked down the road from his home for the last time. I was to visit once more but for different circumstances. I phoned a taxi from the garage at the bottom of the road and went home to a solitary grief.

It was over and it was in fact a good thing, it was never going anywhere. We were two snowbirds who had wintered together, now there were no birds in last years nest. My Father was upset, he had liked Alex and liked having him around. He was sorry for me and told me to go over and buy myself a bottle of wine, which I did.

That night he made our usual last cups of tea but said he would have his in the kitchen, he had a touch of indigestion, we didn't query it, my mind was too occupied and so later we all went to our beds. I lay there for a long time remembering, wishing in a way I had kept Alex's love letters, they were beautiful. He had sent mine back too, we were muddle headed at that time. I went to sleep but at 6am my Mother came into my room and said "Joan, can you come, your Father is not well". When I saw him I knew immediately something was wrong, his cheeks were puffed out and his eyes frightened. I thought it was a stroke, I ran down and phoned a Doctor, I should have called an ambulance but I wasn't thinking straight after everything that had happened to me.

We waited and waited and then I ran down into the street and asked a passer by, a man, where the nearest phone was. I was totally phased by now, there's a Police box just down the road he said, can I help you? But by then I realised I had run right past our own phone and called the ambulance. I went back upstairs. By then Mrs File, our lodger, was also in the room. Her hand over her mouth in worry as I got to the bed my Dad's face went whiter than white, his eyes became a clear clear blue and his head dropped to one side. He's gone Joan, my poor Mum said. Oh god I thought, no more.

The ambulance arrived but they couldn't revive him, by then the Doctor had arrived and he came out and said he had died. His pills were all over the floor and we realised he had dropped them. The ambulance man counted them at the Doctors request and he asked when did he have his last prescription made out. I realised with horror they were suspicious, but when we told them his Doctors name they were satisfied. I picked some flowers from the garden and tucked them into the belt which was round the casket they took my Dad away from us in.

So now there was just Mum and I in that big lovely house.

All our dreams in ashes. Where would we go from here, I couldn't think, I phoned Wanda and she phoned Alex. He said he wouldn't come, he didn't want unpleasantness at a time like this but he sent a beautiful card to both of us, which Mum accepted simply because it was to me as well.

So another funeral. People were very kind and helped us but now there was just Mum and me. Now my sister and Roman were thinking of selling their home and coming to see if they could settle in England, which they did. They stayed in the house with us. My Doctor was worried he thought it would be too tiring for me. But he attended my Sister and Niece when they were poorly. Roman tried to settle in London, his firm had given him a transfer there, but in the end they found it wouldn't work and decided to go back to Canada. My Mother was broken hearted as it would leave us all alone.

Then things began to change, while Roman and Edna were still here, Mazy Kaziu had appeared suddenly from Luton. Roman tried to get him interested in Canada thinking perhaps we would get together and go with Mum over there, no way, I wasn't interested. But Kaziu continued to come down even after the family had gone home. I couldn't have cared less, but one day in September he came and invited me to go and stay with him and his friend, whom he lived with in Luton for a weeks holiday. I didn't want to go, not at all, but he said there is going to be a Polish harvest dance and you can't stay in an ice box of a life forever. Eventually I agreed and made arrangements to meet him on St Pancreas Station where he would drive me to Luton. I made sure he realised it was only as a friend and he agreed.

When we reached the house where he lived with his friend, the friend was just leaving for a night shift at Vauxhall, where he worked. He shook hands and his first words to me were "some people you remember, some you forget, you, I remember". He had been my first guest when I married Ludwik. His name was Stanislaw, Staszek he would be to me. We said cheerio and I went in to meet the other Polish lodger. We had supper and Kaziu showed me my room. It was going to prove difficult where he was concerned and I wedged a chair under the door handle. That's told him, I thought.

We went to the dance which was truly lovely, all the harvest customs, the national costumes and girls carrying sheafs of corn. The Mayor was there and it really was an enjoyable evening. But I had a very empty, lonely feeling inside of me, it should have been Ludwik with me. The week passed pleasantly enough. We were to go down to London to see Fiddler on the roof, although, I would rather have sat in the garden with Staszek, I had rather taken to him. As it was, we went to London for nothing, it wasn't the cast we were expecting to be in it so we went back home. Staszek was being very hospitable, it was his house and I felt quite drawn to him. I was introduced to another Polish family two doors away, Wanda and Josef and they made me very welcome also.

The time came for me to go back home. On the way we hit floods at Redhill and Kaziu suggested we put up at a hotel for the night. No way! A bar tender suggested we leave the car in the station car park and take the train, which we did. So ended my first stay in Staszek's home, I think we both knew I would go back.

The wind had begun to blow in the direction of my future, once again fate had taken a hand. I think we both knew that the next time we met up we would want to get more acquainted with each other. Poor Kaziu, if only he knew.

Kazik

Roman and Edna and the children were still with us but time was passing. In October I went with Kaziu again to Luton. We were going to a dance in Reading. First we were going to friends of his and I thought we had been invited. I was really embarrassed when I realised that they hadn't known we were coming. But they were very welcoming and they were on the committee running the dance. Before we left, it was very clear to Staszek and myself that something was developing between us and I actually couldn't wait for the evening to be over and go back to him. However, the dance was very enjoyable, I danced with a charming young man, I think his name was Stephan, I don't really recall and Kaziu sulked in the bar because I danced mostly with his young man. When we came to drive home, we couldn't find our way out of Reading. We went round and round and eventually a police car drove up and asked if we needed help. They gave us directions but still we got lost, so we had a police escort out of Reading. Great!

When we got home it was in the early hours of the morning,

the milkman was almost due. It was very cold. After we had got into bed, I lay and listened to see if Kaziu had settled, then did something that most people would find a bit out of the ordinary. I crept along to Staszek's room, quietly opened the door and slipped into bed beside him. Just that and only that, he put his arm around me as if to protect me, which if we had but known it he would be doing for many years to come. Just my luck to leave his room as Kaziu was leaving his, oh dear, the fat was really in the fire. But he drove me back to Brighton and even took me back up to Staszek once more after that.

Then I invited Staszek down to us for the weekend. I met him at the station and took him home. Roman set about making him interested in Canada and my small nephew resented the fact that he was there. Why did that guy kiss you? he asked. While Staszek was with us, the inevitable happened. My Mother was quite aware but didn't say a word.

We invited Staszek for Christmas but he didn't want to come, I really don't know why but he said he would phone me. Mum and I went shopping for presents and I found a lovely pair or pyjamas for him, they looked Russian with a high neck and strangely enough he sent me a beautiful powder blue nightgown and matching negligee. I found out afterwards Wanda had chosen them for him. I also sent him a record of the Impossible Dream and one other with Mario Lanza. Then came the time for Roman and Edna to take the family home. Oh god, my poor Mother, she stood in the middle of the road breaking her heart as the taxi took them out of our lives. Would the trauma never end? Actually, Roman had gone on before Edna to prepare a home for them and Edna and the children left just before Christmas. The house felt like a shell. Mrs File had moved, she felt too sad in the house now and the hill was getting too much for her. So at Christmas there were three of us, Mum, Auntie Rose and me. I prepared presents for them and took them in with a cup of tea on Christmas morning, but in truth, nothing could lift us.

It was bitterly cold outside. Mum cooked a traditional lunch which none of us really wanted, we ate in my large beautiful room, how can this be happening was my constant thought. Staszek hadn't phoned which sent my spirits further down and after lunch Mum and Auntie went to sleep. Mouths open and snoring. I sat there until I could take it no more, I quietly dressed and went out for a walk. It was cold, oh so cold, in my body and in my heart. I walked up Preston Park Avenue, there was not a soul in sight, not even a dog or a cat. I walked on, tears running down my cheeks, looking in at the lighted windows where people were enjoying the day. I thought I don't really want to live anymore but I turned my footsteps homeward and Mum and Auntie were watching out for me, worried to death. But a little later Staszek phoned, he said it had snowed deeply and he had been unable to get to a phone, he hadn't got one of this own.

So Christmas passed and somehow we carried on. One day I went to the fish shop and there was a lady chatting to the owner, I gathered she was looking for somewhere to live, not being happy where she was. We now had an empty room and kitchen and I said if you would like to come and see them you will be welcome. Her name was Sue and she was a very pleasant little lady and so we arranged for her to come the next day. She liked the room very much and a bit later she moved in with us, bringing her budgie. This made it easier for me to travel up to Luton to stay with Staszek from time to time. Kaziu decided to move out, quite bitter about how things had turned out and I never saw him again.

Another friend of Staszeks moved in, Walenty, and gradually I stayed longer and longer. Late in 1970 we decided to get married and thought it would be nice on Boxing Day. Mum was going to Canada to Edna for Christmas and I thought it better for her not to be at the wedding. They would all be strangers to her and Josef, Wanda's husband was going to give me away and that would have upset Mum deeply. So that's what we settled on, I went to London and chose a powder blue dress in very fine wool semi mini and with pearls and silver embroidery around the neck and cuffs. I had bought silver shoes and managed to get a pill box shape of hat from one of the hat factories and Wanda covered it in the same blue as my dress. I sewed a little eastern style feather on the side and for something borrowed I had her little fox fur cape. Her two daughters would be bridesmaids and her young son a page boy. Wanda was to do the reception at her home, so everything was set. Christmas night was clear and cold, but when we awoke on my wedding day it was snowing and already deep on the roads. Walenty, our best man had a job to reach us. The flowers had turned up but the florist had left out one of the bridesmaids bouquets and had to go back for it. I was getting very anxious, Staszek and Walenty had gone on ahead. Krystyn went to look out of the window and said there is a man at your front door Janka, but no car. We called him and he said I'm so sorry I can't get up the hill, you will have to walk down. Then he said but you look so lovely I think on second thoughts I will keep you to myself. I was too worried and nervous to appreciate any compliments. I put a mac around me, old shoes on and we walked down to the car. The driver said don't worry they can't start without you, just be sure to change your shoes. I was worried Staszek might come back for us. Then Wanda had forgotten her confetti, never mind said our cheerful driver, you have confetti from heaven, it was still snowing hard, swirling around the car. Finally we arrived and Josef walked me down the aisle, strangely or maybe naturally I felt a little sad. A memory filtered into my mind, in fact more than one. But I made my way to where there were two lovely chairs, side by side in front of the alter for Staszek and I. There was a crib and a Christmas tree and the church was full. We had two Priests and I took my vows in Polish with the gentle second Priest prompting me and then it was over. We walked together from the church, my bridesmaids were feeling the cold in their flimsy dresses. Our cheerful driver helped me into the car and off we went back to Wandas.

At the door we took the traditional bread and salt, I can't quite recall what they signify now but it is a nice custom. Wanda had prepared a beautiful reception. I don't recall a lot about the next couple of hours, my feelings were very mixed, no regrets but my Mum and Dad were absent, I was now exiled as it were to Luton, I felt, yes I felt a little overwhelmed. But finally Joe saw us home a few doors away. There was ice on the pavement and we had to take care. We went to our bedroom and Wanda had covered it with a beautiful white cover and so began my second married life.

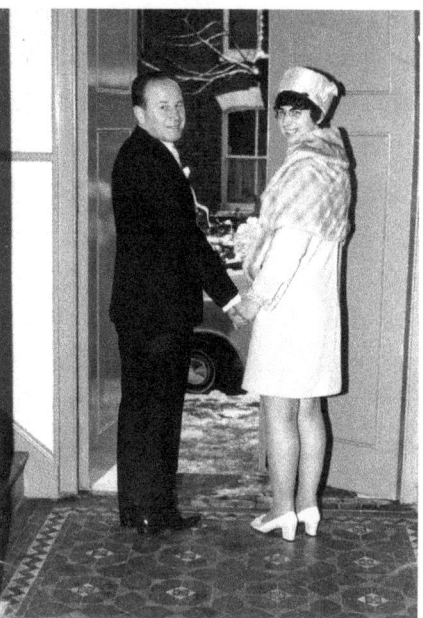

Joan   Joan & Stan's Wedding

I wondered how I would feel in the days to come and thinking I shouldn't have doubts, but things settled down. We had postponed our honeymoon for later in the year in Paris and that was to end with yet another wrenching sadness for me. But that was a little way off yet and when Mum came back from Canada we met her and brought her home with us and dressed in our weddings clothes. We held a reception for her, she didn't seem quite herself, she was very tired and I thought that it was the journey. We enjoyed the evening and Mum went to her room to rest, then she had to go home. By then I had sold the house (or almost) and Mum was living in a flatlet in Beaconsfield Villas run by the Rotary Club. She was not very happy living alone but she didn't want to come to Luton and I think uprooting her would have been too much for her at her age.

Sue was still visiting her and she went to a club, just across the road and seemed to be managing. Now I had sold the house we could think about moving as well and making a fresh start. We moved to an upside down house in Devon Road nearer to where Stan worked. It was quite nice but a little noisy with the factory and airport, but there were shops near and we settled down. Life went on. I wasn't sorry I had married Stan but I was very homesick, I never really liked Luton. My nerves were very bad, everything seemed suddenly to come back to me. I spent hours alone gardening or working in the house, shopping and I cannot say my memories of these times are soft and gentle. I was among comparative strangers. Then we had new neighbours come across the road. A Polish Jew whose name was Tony and his wife Judith. They had a brilliant idea, they invited all their nearest neighbours to a party at their home to get to know them, and it proved to be a great success.

We met Betty and Hugh. Hugh was a professor at the college, also Wendy and Mike and got to know Sheila and Mick our immediate neighbours better. Tony's parties were fab, he was quite a boy, even proposing strip poker. I went only for jewellery but Tony was about to go the whole way until his wife gave him a very obvious warning. But he was great, his music was great and he injected life back into things. I gave a party for all of them also, but somehow my life in Luton never took off. Stan promised me that when he retired we could come back home.

Before all of this, however, we had our honeymoon in Paris, in 1971. We went down to see my Mother just before we went and I was very worried. She had been to the Doctor and something was wrong with her bowel tests, she said we were not to cancel our trip, it had been arranged and I was going to meet Stan's Sister and family. I felt very uneasy, but Sue, bless her, still being a very good friend to my Mum and they both said to go. So we did. First we went to Dunkirk, to Stan's sister and family who gave us a very loving reception. I liked France from the beginning, the food, the whole atmosphere. Life seemed to quicken over there.

Then we went to Paris. We had not booked anywhere to stay and went to a little office that arranged these things. We wanted somewhere near the seine so we could see all the sights. They sent us to a small hotel quite near the river. At first glance the street looked a bit dubious but once inside the hotel it was really plush and soft and hospitable. I enjoyed the continental breakfast and all of the food. We set off to see the sights. I loved the left bank and all the artists working along the riverside. We went to Notre Dame and the Sacre Coeur. We walked in all, 10 miles in the end. I sat down in the church and said to Stan "you carry on, I can't walk another step". But it was wonderful, I loved France, I felt I could lie back into the atmosphere there, I had my photo taken with a Gendarme and we had our silhouettes painted by a riverside artist. It was easy to realise and visualise how half the artists, poets and political rebels had lived in Garrets there, they had left their ghosts walking by the seine, the very air smelt romantic.

But it came, time to go, back to Dunkirk. We had visited Stan's other sister in Collomiers south of Paris and I had enjoyed that as well, very much so. The long fresh crusty loafs that appeared every morning, the pernod aperitif and the delicious food, a barbeque where Stan's nephew had cooked fresh salmon steaks in butter wrapped in foil. Oh yes, I came alive in France.

Now it was time to go home, all sweet times pass like a dream and so quickly, but they live in our hearts to sustain us through difficult times. How soon I was going to find that one true. We boarded the train to Dunkirk, the attendant was telling us something but we didn't understand. Then a man passenger in front of us drew some wagons on a card and marked the front ones as the only ones that were going to Dunkirk. Great!! Instead of going through the train to the right ones before Stan could stop me I grabbed my heavy suitcase and almost ran down the platform to the front carriage. Stan was to say the least exasperated, however, thanks to the kind Frenchman, we were on our way.

We stayed with Julie and Maurice one more night and then set off for home, little dreaming what was going on at home.

As soon as I got in I rang my Mum and asked "how are you Mum?" Not good she answered and I knew. I knew straight away something was very wrong. My Mum never ever was negative. I told Stan I have to go down to my Mother, he had to return to work so I went alone. When I reached my Mother's flat, Sue was there and Mum was about to be going into hospital. I went crazy. Why didn't you let me know I asked. But Mum was past explaining and what hurt more was that she didn't want me to go to the hospital with her, she wanted Sue. Was she after all resenting the fact that we went away? She had urged us to go. So I stood at the window and waved her goodbye just as I had with Ludwik. She looked up as she got into the taxi and I felt alone and awful. Sue, god bless her had gone with her.

She was going to have an operation for cancer of the bowel just as her Father had. I paced her flat and rang Stan who said he would come when he could. Stan was not Ludwik, or even Alex, he clung to his job as if it was his lifeline. I don't blame him, his young life had been very insecure and precarious. So it was Sue and I who slept at her flat in a twin bed in her room, I was glad of her company.

When I went up to see Mum after the op I was told that

the cancer had been inoperable and they were now only interested in keeping her out of pain. The nurse said she had come round just long enough to see my flowers, also those of my childhood friend, Dorothy and her husband, Edek. Bless you Dorothy, I thought. Strangely enough I had taken her Mum flowers a week before she had suddenly died, such are the vagaries of fate or the blessings? The Sister asked me if I wanted Mum to go into a nursing home and I replied "Sister it would be better were she to be taken than suffer like this" and Mum in a nursing home would have suffered, I would have had to go back up to Stan.

The Sister turned to the Nurse and gave her a small glass of medicine and said give this to Mrs Long at 8pm. Mum reacted badly to pain killers but it was the only merciful thing to do, they couldn't leave her in pain. So Sue said to Mum, goodnight my love, god bless. I just left, I couldn't take anymore.

We went to bed and I slept fitfully. At 6am the next morning the telephone rang in the downstairs flat, I knew, I got out of bed and put a dressing gown on. Our doorbell rang, I opened it and said to the young man "I know! I know!" and for some reason thanked god all the way back up to Sue, no more suffering, but now there was another emptiness inside me.

I phoned Stan and he said he would come straight down. What a beginning to our married life, straight back from Paris to the agony of loss and the ending of an era.

A friend of Romans, Edwin, phoned Canada for me to tell my Sister, forgetting to them it was the middle of the night, they were not very pleased, until told and shock set in. It seemed to me by now that funerals were a way of life. I still couldn't cry, the Policewoman was right I was paying for not doing so when I lost Ludwik. Stan cried at the funeral but I couldn't and I don't remember much about this one. I just remember my Aunt catching my hand from behind me and telling me they were there, then the finality of the curtains closing. Then we went back to Sue's, she was very good to us and helped as much as she could.

Then came the clearing of Mum's flat. I can't remember much, a furniture dealer took it. I remember Mum's rocking chair going, she loved that thing, I suppose it was a comfort. All I kept were some tiny chipmunks she had bought from Canada, a Mother and babies. I still have them, they sit a few steps from where I am writing this.

So, back to Luton to try to resume a normal life. It was not life as I had always known it, it was strange to feel that no matter which direction I walked in, I should not come to the sea, I felt a bit trapped.

It was nice that Tony had acquainted us with folk around us, I was not quite so lonely and we gathered from time to time. Betty and Hugh gave a burns night. Hugh was a Scot with pipes and haggis! and we all had to recite one of Robbie Burns' poems. I gave a cheese and wine party, things like that. But somehow my heart was never quite in it. Slowly my nerves were once again beginning to suffer. I had registered with Stan's Doctor, a Dr Crarer. He was very kind and tried to help me, but as I hadn't given him my past, it was difficult. Then one day I received the news my Aunt had died and I really was in a bad way then. I called the surgery and they said the Doctor would call. I was alone and as the morning wore on I was getting really out of it. I called the surgery again and the receptionist said do you have someone with you Mrs Malek to make you a cup of tea? When I said no she said Dr Crarer will be with you in a few minutes and true to her word, he was, as he came in his bleeper was still going.

He sat in a chair opposite me and after three months of not telling him anything I told him all that had happened since Ludwik. He sat up straight. "Jesus Christ" he said, "no wonder you are ill, why haven't you talked to me before?". He said a lot of his patients could have been helped earlier, if they only told him everything.

From then on he helped me a lot, him and Dr Tabbart who understood quite deeply about circles of stress having to be broken. They doped me quite heavily and when Stan and I went to Poland to meet his family for the first time I nearly fell off a chair after unwisely having a vodka. I can't imagine what they thought of me.

But our first visit was lovely, in spite of it all they gave me a wonderful welcome and accepted me as their own. My elderly Mother-in-law eyed me a little curiosity. To her I suppose I was a foreign wife, but we got on well enough. I could speak pigeon Polish and the children had great fun explaining things to me. The family lived on the land, a quite large expanse of land, a farm in the middle of the forests. I was in my element and I started to pick up in my health. All fresh food, home produced. Chickens running everywhere, a cow, Mary brought into milk morning and night and wild cats used to come and sit in the stable waiting for a drink.

There were village weddings which went on for three days. At night I would lay and listen to the music coming over the sweet scented summer air. We were invited to one, we danced in the open air and I learned all the customs which were quite lovely. Fireflies danced in among the trees, there was a huge yellow moon and the smell from the trees of the forest was so fresh. I really thrived feeling free and loved. I liked the Polish cuisine and put on weight too.

Then it was time to come back to Luton. Our visit was over and back to work for Stan, I was lonely once again. Off and on for all the eleven years I lived there my nervous trouble would rear its head. I always had a sensitive nature right from a child and the doctor would ask my Mother, do you have anyone in the country to send her to and I would go to my Aunt Betty, Mum's Sister and my cousins for schooling on doctors orders.

So now when I was home, sick and often on my own at night when Stan did night shifts, I grew nervy again and more tablets. Stan promised that when he retired we could move back to Brighton and that was to be sooner than we thought.

After a time I found myself a job, not long before Christmas but I couldn't get one in toys. My last try was at the Co-Op, I filled in a form thinking my age would hinder me but the lady who interviewed me set a time for me to come in and see the manager. When I told Stan, however, he didn't want me to do full time so out of politeness I rang the Co-Op to tell them I wouldn't be coming. Right at the last minute she said "Oh just a minute Mrs Malek we have a part time job going in menswear". I had had some experience with that so I jumped at it, it was from Monday until Wednesday. Fine I said I would love to do that.

So at least I got out and met people. I picked a dreadful winter to do it though, I had to wear socks over my shoes and walk to work half an hour at least over the ice bound roads and streets. The bus had slowed to one side half way down the hill.

It was a break for me to meet people and extra cash and so we went on.

One day Betty rang me and said "congratulations!" I said"

what for I haven't had a baby." She said (I nearly dropped the phone) "you have a Polish Pope, Pope John Paul the Second." I couldn't believe it, the first non Italian Pope in about four hundred years. I couldn't wait for Stan to come home but, he already knew. We were delighted. Imagine what the Poles in Poland must have been thinking and feeling, this was a patent for many major happenings. Then one day at work our manager came running on to the floor and said "someone has shot the Pope". I clung to the counter and nearly passed out. Who? said the manger, would harm a gentle, holy man like that. We were all in an awful state, until we knew he was going to live. Things would never be the same for him, physically again, but we had him back. I forgive him said Pope John Paul and when he recovered, he was to often visit the man that did it in his prison cell.

Time went on and in 1982 our relations in France wrote and said they would like to come and visit us with their new little two month old son, Sebastian. It was Stan's niece and her husband Francois. I bought as much French style food as I could, prepared their room and felt quite elated that they were coming. We had a lovely time with them, took them up to Luton too, where the czars grandaughter lived, pushed the baby round there and nursed him at home, it was lovely. Then came the time for them to go home, I should miss hearing Francois in the morning saying bonjour bebe.

After they had gone I stripped the bed and washed the linen and whilst doing it I felt very sore under my bust. When I looked I had open sores. Oh God I thought, cancer. I felt quite bad the next day, stayed in bed and called Dr Crarer. That's shingles he said. I can promise you a bit of pain with that! Thanks I thought! He gave me some extra strong pain killers and I was home for seven weeks. I had been afraid for

Sebastian but, no said the Doctor you can't catch shingles. Thank God for that.

We were in 1982 and the Pope was coming to England. He was coming to Crystal Palace football ground, I was only just recovered from my spots, but this I would not miss.

We had to catch the coach at 4am down in Luton and Kaziu Kazan slept over thus in order to drive us to the pick up spot. It was very cold and I was weak as yet, but I couldn't wait. We got there and we found our seats. There were Poles from all over England, block by block of seats housed different towns, sure enough we were right next to the Brighton block but didn't know it until we left. I sat shivering a bit, but so overwhelmed by the visit and when that helicopter came clattering overhead, my heart raced so fast it nearly left me. The roar of cheering and singing that broke out as Pope John Paul landed was deafening. Oh the joy, to have him there with us, a mass I will never forget. His deep rich warm voice was so different as to when on the TV and its hard to describe the wonderful togetherness of us all. When it came time for him to leave there was a chorus of please don't leave us and as the Pope mobile drove around the track with Pope John Paul smiling and waving goodbye, a terrific chorus broke out of a mountain song from the area he came from. It says Gural are you not sad to leave us, return, come back. Gural being the name for someone from the mountain region. I was sobbing as he left, as were many many more and then there was the emptiness, yet he had left a spiritual warmth with us all.

So our momentous moments were over and we walked over to talk with Dorothy and our other friends from Brighton. Had I but known it, the Popes visit had put my feet on the path that lead back to Brighton. We chatted and I said to Dorothy "why don't you come up for a visit to us Dolly," and she replied, "that would be nice, we can make arrangements later for that," so we left it open.

I think it was about august, we were to get together at our home. I really looked forward to it, if I had known the outcome of my friends visit, I would have been really sitting on hot coals!

The day arrived and we met Dorothy. I'm not sure of the bus or train, but anyway, we were together. Chatter for a while was non-stop, cosy as we sat in the evening, Dolly in her curlers and dressing gown, little moments of sadness and a tear as we talked about her loss and her beloved husband Edek. But we enjoyed taking her up to Luton Hoo the home of the Czar's grandaughter, I can't surprisingly recall her name, but it is a beautiful place in contrast to industrial Luton. I used to love going up there, I don't believe I cannot remember her name. But the week soon passed and Dorothy said, little realising what it would spark in me, "why don't you and Stan come back to live in Brighton." Bang! it had hit me, Stan had promised once he retired we would go back. Stan had already taken a voluntary settlement from his work in Vauxhall, retired by taking part of a lump sum and part in a small pension, redundancy is the word I'm looking for. So why not, well, strike why the irons hot I thought. Dorothy had told us that there was a house for sale in the street where her sister lived, Ashford Road, it sounded very inviting. So after putting Dorothy on the bus for home, we crossed the road, oh yes, in every sense, to the estate agents and put our house on the market. That was on the Saturday Dolly had said we could stay with her if we went down to visit.

All day Sunday I dreamed and hoped. Monday morning the agent phoned and said could she bring a couple to see the house?... oh yes she could! I couldn't wait for their arrival and reaction. The young man came into the lounge first and called out to his lady, come and look at this. By the tone of his voice, I thought and my heart started to beat fast, its going to be the same as when we sold Stan's, a first viewing winner, and it was.

Now it was panic stations, we had to get to Brighton and view the one near Lar, ask Dolly if we could stay. My usual nervous reactions set in, I always did want everything yesterday so to speak. But Dolly agreed, it was a bit sudden for her and I think inconvenient but bless her she said it was ok to come. So we took more steps towards home. We settled in at Dolly's then, I think, she went with us to the house in Ashford Road. I wasn't caught by its appearance, the lady of the house had a lot of stone cladding over the fire place and in the corner, it was, to me, a rather weird room. However, one could always alter that. She asked if we had to sell a house ourselves to buy and without thinking, so eager was I to come home I said no. A classic fib which would rebound on us later. However, we notified Mr Coles, our Solicitor, he didn't think my fit was a very good idea but anyway things had begun.

Dorothy's young daughter, Christine, did kindly take us to see a few other places but nothing appealed and Ashford Road was near the shops, Post Office etc and Lar was just along the road, familiar to me.

So we returned to Luton to find a sold board had been put up. That really should have been a for sale one, in case things fell through. Our neighbours were a bit upset we hadn't said anything but I explained we didn't know ourselves until three days ago. Somehow things progressed, I made what seemed like a scroll of things to do, book removals, change electric and gas over to Brighton, oh millions of things. My nervous system was beginning to feel the strain. Everything seemed in a fog anyway, the buyers didn't seem to be moving very fast with their end. However we had enough money just to buy ours, after that it would be in the lap of the gods.

So the stage was set, we arranged to stay at Sues who was still our good friend, for the night, the van would pack our things, travel down and meet us at the house the morning after. I began to feel tired and a little sick it all seemed so much to do and I had realised that there would be no Mum or Dad to greet us now, just my wide open Brighton, beloved mine and friends who had probably grown apart from me after all this time. So Pope John Paul and Dorothy had brought my dream true , it would not be the same, one can never go back, as a Greek philosopher had once written, you can't put your feet in the same river twice, but I was going home to memories, familiar streets and were I but to know it a lot more.

I can't recall things in sequential order so much water has passed under the bridge since then but I remember Sue had a meal ready for us when we arrived, the van went off the following morning and so we began our life back in Brighton. I expect Staszek felt a little sad, he had left all his friends behind now and had yet to make new ones. For the moment though we were going to be busy. The morning dawned and I sat in front of the mirror in Sue's room actually terrified of leaving her and going to the stone age room in Ashford Road, but we had to do it. So we stood at the front door, I don't even recall the number of the house and soon, along came the van. Further along the road Lar ran down her path and waved to us which eased the nerves in my tummy.

Soon everything was moved in and the van departed and we were on our own. We went into the back garden and the grass in the house next door was knee high. Apparently the lady was in hospital having a hip replacement. The first thing I had to do was to go around to the shops to buy some food etc. there were quite a few and a bank a few yards down, not that we had anything to put in there as yet, the money had still not come through from Luton. All we had was our two small pensions, we were spent out buying the house so we had two houses and no cash. I was selling things but somehow we managed. I was paying for the fib I had used to get down here.

There were storage heaters in the rooms and when they went off for a while it was quite chilly. I wasn't keen on the imitation gas fire, I felt small niggling doubts going through my mind, but, I was home. Not long before Christmas, thank heavens. The money finally came through.

I went to the fish shop in the block of shops in Preston Drove to order a duck for Christmas but, he shut shop not long before Christmas so I had to re-order at the butchers, Barfields, it was a lucky buy, the meat was excellent there and the owner Ray was to serve us for years and become a friend. I never used the multi stores, I hated them and always would, I brought all fresh food from the little shopping centre.

I can't really remember that Christmas, I absolutely can't. But I do remember one happy day when I came back from the shops to find a lady sitting there in the lounge. She said John said to come and say hello and I have. It was Margaret, a Dutch lady who used to go to John, my hairdresser long ago. I was so pleased we were going to have her and her husband, Ted, for neighbours, someone we knew. Gradually Stan began to put the combined lounge and dining room right. Oh how hard he had to work.

One day I came back from the shops and he had knocked and pulled the stone down from over the fire place, how he did it

I don't know. He was standing knee deep in dust and broken stone, it was so heavy, I sometimes wonder if he harmed himself even as far back as that. The next thing was knocking out the stone platform in the corner, underneath were dozens of house bricks. "What idiot did that" said Stan, which on repeating that to Margaret I found out it was her son, Peter. Whoops, each to his own I thought.

Then Stan went up to a stone masons in Hartington Road and on a trolley brought home a stone mantle shelf that matched the fire place, how he did that I will also never know. But now I had a second stone fireplace and it brought it back into proportion it looked quite nice. He decorated everywhere and built new walls in the garden and a garden shed that Margaret said looked like a little wooden church. From then on it began to look like home.

Other things were happening while all this was going on. My nerves were very unsteady and one day I thought I would brave it and go to the hairdressers round the corner called "Toppers", little did I know how that would affect my future.

I asked if it was possible for me to have my hair cut and a young lady said yes would I take a seat. I sat watching a very attractive girl doing someone's hair and suddenly she glanced across at me and asked if I would like a cup of tea, which I appreciated, I was feeling really strung out.

That same girl did my hair and we got chatting and for some reason I found myself telling her about Ludwik and I told her how someone had said to me think yourself lucky it was not a divorce which I found very strange. It's very true though you know, said this lovely young girl and we talked quite a bit about it. I found I was relaxing with her and when we said goodbye I made my next appointment.

In the following days I thought a lot about her, her name was Lynne and there was something about her that made me want to chat with her again. That, I was to do then and for all the rest of my life. That chance meeting brought me a trusting friendship that carried so much for me over the years, but that is yet to come.

At about this time things started to get better. It started on one fine sunny day, Stan and I were walking down Cleveland Road thinking to go to Preston Park when I noticed a quite beautiful flowering shrub in one of the gardens. We stood looking wondering what it was. Suddenly the door opened and a gentleman about our age came out, he smiled at us and I explained that we were wondering what the flowers were. He told us I believe, it was Jasmine but I can't really remember, what I did take note of was his accent, I was sure I recognised it. I asked him in Polish if he were a Pole, he was really delighted, yes he answered are you? I told him Staszek was and they shook hands. In the space of five minutes we were seated in his dining room and were introduced his wife, Josephine. His name was Ludwik and a cup of tea was set before us. That was about the fastest acquaintance we had ever made. We chatted for quite a time and Ludwik mentioned that they always went to Sunday mass at St Mary's where long ago I had been confirmed. We said we would see them there on the coming Sunday and left.

Sure enough on Sunday we met after mass and were introduced to an Italian lady, Lina and her husband, George who was a Pole. She spoke perfect Polish, put me in the shade! We all walked up Preston Drove together, stopped at the top of Cleveland Road and chatted. Suddenly a man came down the path of the house where we were chatting and Ludwik and Josephine said to him, "why were you not at church?" "I don't have time for church" he said, I thought he is just kidding. However, we were introduced and his name was Edmund, yet another one of our Polish clan.

The following Sunday sure enough there he was with his wife at mass, her name was Sheila. So from gazing at flowers in someone's garden on a sunny afternoon, was born a friendship that was to last quite a while. After that we used to go to each others homes after church for a coffee, a drink and happy conversation. The year went around and at Christmas Edmund invited us in on the way home. He had a beautiful tree, every year he said, he went into the country to the gypsies for his tree. By then our own home was looking fine, our garden had flowers and we settled down.

For about five years I was quite healthy. Edmund organised picnics, theatre visits and we went to Polish dances at the Hove Town Hall. Mike and a friend were trying to raise enough money to fund a Polish club, which eventually they did. One could go there for lunch after Polish mass on Sundays. I joined a poetry circle which I really enjoyed, Stan would read his own peaceful read, or do whatever jobs he wanted to do so we were both happy. Margaret next door introduced us to another Pole who lived at the end of our road, his Wife was French and she had not long lost her daughter. Margaret told them about us and one day they came to see us. Micheline gave me a box of ferrero rocher and we had quite a nice chat.

So our social life was really quite happy and busy. That all lasted up until 1988, the last year that things went well. Edmund became ill, although he never gave into it, he remained cheerful always. Sheila also had nervous trouble like me, Josephine was poorly and the wind of change turned cold. We had a wonderful Deacon at our church, Peter, and he visited everybody and was so gentle and kind. Then we had trouble also, Margaret moved out to a flat and we had really noisy neighbours move in, a real horror for me.

In 1989 my Sister, Edna and Roman came over to stay with us for a couple of weeks which was lovely. When they came I was having lessons with a Polish lady, a dear friend of mine, Stella. Roman looked at my books and said you know this is dam difficult, for it was the grammar I was learning. I had been going to her for quite a while, I enjoyed our afternoons very much. Her Sister, who was a nun and another little nun, Sister Margaret, used to sit doing embroidery or making rosaries and Stella and I would work at my lessons. Afterwards I really enjoyed her home made doughnuts, paczki, they were called, pronounced ponchki.

Life was a mixture of sadness and joy for a while. Then my nerves began to go because of the continuous racket next door, I was back with Dr Myers and he had me assessed for a Counsellor. He was a nice young man, very astute and helpful. I used to hate being in my home because I could never rest there.

I must tell of a happening that occurred several years back because it had a bearing on all that was to come. One day not long after we came back to Brighton, Lar had phoned me and said she wasn't well, could I go along and ring for a Doctor. So I went along and did just that. We didn't have to wait long, the door bell rang and I opened the door to a tall very personable young Doctor, he was very kind to Lar and I stayed while he examined her. Then he wrote a letter, sealed it and asked me if I could make sure she went to the A&E at the Sussex County. I would take her he said but I have to see another patient. I would take her! I thought, I was impressed. When he had gone I said to Lar if Dr Myers ever retires that's the

Doctor I want, she didn't even tell me he was at my surgery. She wanted to give me some money for helping her, no way, but she kept insisting so I said in the Co-Op there is a lovely white bear I would like so I did just that and bought it and to this day it sits on my bed, a few years later I was to remember that day.

So here we were, a few years later, I was really ill with my nerves, the young man who was helping me did truly help me with many things. I couldn't believe I had come back to this state again, we had had some lovely years. Edmund had organised picnics that were truly old fashioned and lovely. We would wander in the woods, find somewhere to set our picnic, lounge, chat and enjoy. We sat at the edge of the woods, forest, I used to call it with the last soft sun rays touching the trees and grass and watch the rabbits come out to the verge, so peaceful.

Roman, Joan, Edna & Stan

Stan and I had been to Canada, Vancouver to be exact, a beautiful place and really spent a great vacation with them. We would go out for breakfast, for blueberry muffins and coffee, the people were so pleasant. On Canada day we went up the mountain "whistler" to the little village half way up, one would see the occasional brown bear sitting by the side of the path. I had my photo taken, we all did with the tall mountains and I had one with an Indian Chief with his cloak wrapped around us. There was Indian dancing and it was all lovely. Further up the mountain it was very very cold, my brother-in-law had worked out an itinery for the whole three weeks, for wet or dry weather. His Sister, Martha said there hadn't been a storm for almost six years. I am petrified of storms. Sure enough I had just undressed for bed and there was one hell of a clap of thunder, it reverberated around the mountain. I never dressed again so quickly in my life, my sister who had never been nervous, even of the bombs, found that very funny.

We went to a place where salmon came in to spawn and die. We watched through the glass window as they swarm in, in their thousands. Imagine all the babies that would grow and go thousands of miles, maybe in the ocean and return each year to the very same place, how wonderful is life and nature. One day I remember and will always remember we went to a place called Chekamoose and climbed the rocks high over a rushing river. I suddenly felt every ounce of tension leave me, I was free and light and happy and felt liberated. If only I could have kept that. Further up, Roman had seen a lovely butterfly on the rocks a solitary little creature and photographed it. Its all I have of that moment out of time for me.

Joans happiest moment

Then came the time to fly home, the flight was horrific, we had to discharge fuel and land in Calgary to check the plane, some passengers didn't want to board it again. I went to the desk and asked if we could be put up for the night and take another plane. I'm sorry she said it is the occasion of the Calgary stampede, everywhere is booked. I stood my ground and she said, If I bring the pilot will that help, which she did. Mam he said, I got a wife and two kids back home, I wouldn't fly it if it wasn't safe. So on we went to Toronto and spent the day in a beautiful hotel at their, the airlines, expense.

Finally, at midnight we boarded the same plane, then there

was a seat belt missing, two people were required to right that, and last of all a passenger missing, so all the luggage was unloaded and searched in a bomb scare! Finally, we left, leaving (I might add) some of the unfortunate passengers luggage left behind, not ours though, or I would have raised Cain. I thought, we have to cross the Atlantic in this ancient jalopy, but at least Stan and I were together and I felt under our seats for life belts. On the Friday of that week the airline went broke so we were comparatively lucky.

So life moved on, the poetry class split up, Margaret had moved, the house next door was a nightmare of noise and so I began the downward trend.

One day Mike came and said "I'm sorry Joan I have a little bad news, Dr Myers is retiring and I want to take you down to say goodbye to him. We don't want another sadness to stay with us." I must make a point here. Whilst I was still with Dr Myers, I had had a very bad day with my breathing and it continued after I went to my bed. We called the surgery and soon the bell rang, a tall doctor came into my room and said just four words "you really mustn't panic". I remember my mind tuned into his voice and I remember saying "please don't leave me like this" and he gave me a large duck egg size pill. I took it and I remember saying "oh I feel so good" and was out like a light. But I remembered in the morning so I was prepared for what would come when I said goodbye to my Dr Myers after so many years.

When Mike and I went into the surgery, Dr Myers stood up and said "I had so hoped to see that smile again" and I said "well you've taken care of that now! He came round the desk and said embracing me, "Joan, its time to go," it hurt, it really hurt. This man had been so gentle and kind to me for years, so patient but he said to Mike who does Joan want to go to.

With no hesitation I said "I would like Lar's Doctor" please. "Good" said the doctor, "I will ask him and talk to him Joan. I can't promise he will take Stan but I will have a word."

So we parted. Why is life always partings? Stupid question, natures course but I'm not built for it. I'm not sure I want to be that hard anyway, I wouldn't have enjoyed the good times and beauty so deeply. So we went back home and Stan and I would be going to meet our new doctor. There is one funny story of something that happened while I was still with Dr Myers. I had just come away from the surgery and I was walking up the avenue towards home and out of the blue I thought I've had enough of pills. I was on Ativan at that point, so I decided I was going to stop them there and then. Big mistake. The next night, quite late I started shaking, we were in bed, it got gradually worse and Stan phoned the doctor who told him simply, "make her a cup of tea." Stan straight away dialled 999 and I was taken to hospital in a terrible state, I was put into a bed with rails around it and rattling from head to toe. It was the middle of the night, dead quiet, all the walls around me were white, tiled as I remember, just like a morgue. I was scared silly. "Is there anyone there?" I called into the silence. A man's voice answered "what'd you want?" Oh my god was my first thought, a man has broken in, I'm going to be raped. The trembling stopped abruptly, not even gradually and I climbed over the rails and found a nurse's office. "What are you doing?" she asked. I said there is a man out there. "I know" she said, "poor chap has broken his collar bone skating and is waiting to go upstairs" and she took me back to my bed. I begged her not to leave me. A bit later she came and fetched me into their office until the doctor came. Poor man he couldn't help laughing when the nurse told him about my encounter with the other patient. But he said "don't ever give pills up all at once, I won't give you anything now , you won't thank me tomorrow but I'm keeping you the night to make sure you haven't damaged your heart. So they phoned Stan, explained and I was sent home.

Early the next day Dr Myers came , he said "I won't make you take the tablets" and then he said something I still find funny, though I didn't at the time. He was such a gentleman it was surprising and funny, but he said, "if anyone tells you to pull yourself together, tell them to .... sod off." Good advice really, would one suffer if they didn't have to? But Stan had to smile, he said, "who would have thought that would happen." He saw the doctor to the door and I heard my Doctor say, "I don't give my patients something they don't want, but call me if you need me. So there are funny moments even in this situation and I can remember many.

But now we were beginning anew, it was farewell and hello. We sat in front of the Doctors desk side by side. When the interview was over I said "I'm not worried now you have taken us both". No problem said the doctor and went on writing. I signalled to Stan we should go, but I knew instinctively I had made the right choice.

Mike continued to visit me, he took me to the dentist and also up to Ludwik's grave to try and bring everything I was carrying out. Then even worse was to come. Edmund died, kind sociable Edmund, who had brought so much pleasure to our lives. Mike said "I want you to go to his funeral Joan or afterwards you will regret it." But by now my nerves were so bad I was terrified to go outside. However, Mike said he would come to us on the day so that I could go if I changed my mind.

The day dawned and I dressed suitably in case I could brave it and Mike came, I had my slippers on, but my shoes ready in front of me should I go. Mike sat in the armchair reading a newspaper glancing now and then at me and then the clock. Suddenly I stepped into my shoes and said "I want to go." I put my coat on and clung to Mike as we went out to the car. Stan had already gone to the church. I said "if we get there and I don't want to go in there will you bring me home," yes said Mike, what patience he had.

The hearse was standing outside the church and I said "Edmund is here and I am here, lets go into mass." So we went in, a friend saw me and said "come and sit with us Joan, we also feel bad today." I did and I sang the hymns, I went to communion and surprised Mike, I think. When we came out he said "do you want to go to the cemetery." I said "yes ,but I have to wee first." Oh dear when I remember these things I did and said, but Mike had a friend nearby and rang the bell and asked if I could be accommodated, "please come in" she said.

So we went to the cemetery, Stella was there and for some reason I sang a little Polish hymn for her. Then we went back to Edmunds home, Mike came in for a while and then soon we had to go home. He had given me a lot of time. When he left the feeling was desperately empty, Edmund had gone, taking all those lovely days with him, all just memories now.

So this was the pattern of life for a while, the house next door had become a nightmare on top of which Stan developed a hernia. Our new Doctor made an appointment for him at the hospital, I was scared witless but now I had to think of him. He was getting a lot of pain and I phoned the surgery, My Doctor wrote to us and said he would do his best to help him and soon he had an earlier appointment to go into hospital. They rang up and told us he could now come in on the following day, but I had to ring up on the day to confirm they had a bed, a right tussle developed when they said at the last minute they hadn't one. I told them I am a sick woman and my doctor won't be very impressed with this. Ten minutes later they rang and said bring him in. So I did, I felt terrible leaving him there.

That night I was alone and at 3am in the morning there was an awful thunder storm. I drank a glass of whisky to dull my fear but I was worried about Stan, he knew how scared I was. However time as ever moved on. I rang up the next day to ask how it went and they said, "he's fine, he's in the recovery ward, do you want to speak to him?" Did I just! Stan's sleepy voice came over the phone, "It's all over! he said, I cried with relief. When he came home Mike helped me nurse him and wouldn't let me see the wound. So another trauma over, for anyone in a less nervous state, it would perhaps not have been so bad, but I was really ill now.

But all things pass slowly, through days when I couldn't breathe and felt dizzy with fear, on to an easing of the tension, I had all sorts of help which our Doctor had arranged. Oh how I blessed the day I had called him for Lar long ago, or so it seemed, a lifetime. He was our support at every juncture and one day he managed to encourage me to go down to the surgery. How I did it I don't know, I only knew I wanted to please him and justify everything he had done for us.

I got ready and clutching a crucifix In my hand so tight it left marks. I went with Stan down to the surgery. Well done said my doctor and from them on I started slowly to pick up, I went round to the shops holding on to the wall as I went. I went into Lynne, our lovely hairdresser friend, she had been wonderful when we were ill and used to come to the house to do our hair. Things had been awful, I had spent a day in a hospital ward for mental illness, but wouldn't stay, that was brought on by the noise next door.

Finally I made up my mind to get out of our house and move. Soon would begin another era. Stan agreed that it would be a good idea to move and we contacted the house agents near us, then began the search for something suitable. The agent had told us that 75% of people selling were doing so because of neighbours, we were already living in a noisy age and worse. Each time we viewed we glanced at the next door neighbours on both sides.

One house we looked in was a shambles and I began to lose heart. I walked the streets looking for sale boards everywhere. One day looking for houses for sale in the paper I spotted one in Coldean Lane and mentioned it to Stan. We didn't act on it straight away but after more fruitless searching Stan one day suddenly called out from the kitchen "there is that one on Coldean Lane". We agreed to check it out. I phoned the agent and he told me the number, 21 and we were talking about Bessie's house. It hit me with a shock. I realised it could mean that Bess had succumbed to her illness. I asked the agent would he mind if I phoned back later, of course not, he said. I phoned Janet who had bought number 20 from us many years before and I told her who I was. She confirmed Bessie had died a couple of months back. I told her we were thinking of coming out there and she said " wouldn't mind having you as neighbours." So I rang the agent back, we made an appointment to view and so it began. I walked around Bessie's home, memories besieging me from every corner. Stan had visited Bess with me some time before, so had been in the house, we both liked it. I felt a bit sad and tearful as I saw some knitting Bess had left behind and her rocking chair in the conservatory. Oh how many memories came flooding back. But I had to rein in and be practical. It had gas central heating and I was paranoid about gas, however, the agent told me the boiler was out in the old coal house and it was a very practical system.

So now the negotiating. I wanted it taken down a certain sum and the agent said he would contact the family and let me know by the evening, I could imagine how surprised they would be that I wanted to buy it. By evening Alan had contacted the whole family and they were delighted and the reduction was made. Eveline, the youngest who used to sit on the step watching Ludwik paint said "there was no one she would rather have it." So the wheels were put in motion, someone soon purchased ours, although we heard afterwards she sold again after only 18 months. After the agent left we found Janet on her step, she invited us in for a drink and we had a lovely chat. I noticed the beautiful lawn my Ludwik had laid with a spirit level was still being kept immaculate and I was happy about that. Janet's husband had died, so she was all alone and I think she liked the idea of us coming next door. So we moved in, after all these years it felt really like coming home. The shops at the bottom of the lane were still there, most of them. There was a Post Office not far away to collect our pensions.

But there, as always Stan had a lot of decorating to do. I was scared silly with the gas central heating but Janet phoned Teddy, Bessie's eldest son and he came and explained it all to me and I soon settled down, preferring it actually to electric. But I kept my electric cooker. When we were going to begin decorating after Stan had gone out for something I thought, I'll just see how easy the wallpaper will come off. Shock, the plaster came away with it. Bessie had used industrial wallpaper with heavy paste, what's more she had painted over it which is taboo and it had never really dried. When I tried to move my settee, it had stuck to the wall, funny if not exasperating. So once again Stan had a really difficult job. The dining room had to be totally re-plastered, but the lounge had paint on the walls under the paper, so not so bad. Poor Stan, how many homes had we put right. However we persevered, after the usual stand up fight over colours.

One day up the ladder painting the hall ceiling Stan dropped the pot of white paint! Where that paint managed to reach and cover!! Well first Stan had to strip, he was covered in it and I washed him down with fairy liquid, a detergent. If someone had rung the bell it would have seemed like the goon show. Then I tackled the carpet. Soon I'd had great success, the air was still blue with what Stan had thought and expressed about it. However, onwards we went, Soon once again our home was as we wanted it. Then I invited Deacon Peter to bless the house. Ludwik, Josephine and I think, Sheila came and I put a white lace cloth on the coffee table for our little meal. Peter walked around the house, Stan following with the little container of Holy water. So now the house was really ours.

We had met the people from the other side of us, the husband had very kindly offered to lend us any tools or things we might need.

So life began. Stan loved wondering over the woods, it reminded him of home. I became very friendly with the Indian family that ran the little stores at the bottom of the lane, I bought almost everything from there. Later on in life they were to prove to be very good friends indeed.

Mick the milkman would leave many things I needed and at Christmas would supply a Christmas cake, mince pies etc. My nerves were still very bad though and I still had counselling from access. I was never very steady for long, the smallest thing would upset me, too much had occurred over the years. We went to church at St Francis but I must admit I missed my own parish. Peter often visited us but things were never to be the same. I was constantly having to consult my doctor who never ever failed me, though I'm sure I was a bit trying at times. He was always kind, reassuring and somehow solving things. Our friends used to visit us and sometimes we went to them. But Edmund wasn't there anymore with all his bright innovations. I was put on to three monthly injections of B12.

Then one fatal day Stan and I were sitting together and I could hear a humming noise. I said to Stan where is that noise coming from, but he said he couldn't hear it. I went all over the house and finally it dawned, I was the only one that could hear it. To say I panicked would put it mildly. I was glad when the sound of traffic drowned it. I went down to the doctors but my doctor wasn't there and I saw a lady doctor. Probably with the best of intentions she said "oh that's tinnitus, you've got that for life, you'll have to listen to music etc". I came out on the street and I weaved my way across the road. How I didn't get killed I don't know. I went up to see my Lynne at her hairdressing shop and she said people often get a buzzing in their ear. But I was having none of it, I was literally terrified. I could never live with this I would go crazy. I made an appointment with my own doctor and he did a lots of tests with tuning forks etc and he said "oh, you don't have tinnitus, probably an infection in the inner ear." But he sent me to a specialist, he said I had it. I went back to my doctor with Stan absolutely crazy by now. I remember holding my ears and saying to the doctor I can't go home doctor, I can't I'll go mad and my doctor wise and cool simply said "you can stay here, someone will be here over the lunch hour". I think he was trying to arrange a visit to Neville Road hospital. I remember lunchtime when he had to go and make calls, I begged him not to leave me, when I remember I feel so embarrassed now but he took it all so calmly. I had even asked the receptionist if they had any brandy. She said you can have water Joan, tea or coffee, brandy you don't get. I imagine she never forgot that episode. When evening came I was sent by taxi to the hospital, Neville Road. The lady doctor prescribed tablets for me, eight a day, to keep me quiet. Still my doctor maintained it was not tinnitus. We checked, or rather he did, all over to see if the pills I'd been on for blood pressure could cause it. There were only two cases and anyway I had stopped mine long before.

Then one day it actually stopped, it stopped, oh the blessed peace. My doctor over all the others had been right, he had kept me going all through that agony. It was possibly stress related. I'm a funny make up as he had found out long before. I never ceased to be grateful to him for his faith in his own judgement and skill and doggedness. The agony was over, but what it had done to my frame and nervous system, lingered on long afterwards.

Poor Stan he had a lot to put up with but he was so grateful to our doctor and trusted him until the end of his days. I can't remember a lot about the days and weeks that followed but slowly I recovered, my pills were cut down and Stan had a period of peace, I think.

Through all this my beloved Lynne had stayed with us, coming to do our hair, I can't remember exactly at what point her son Dani was born, I think I was still in Ashford Road. I used to knit for him and we exchanged Christmas gifts etc. I know she was always there for us. One day she brought Dani out to see us, around Easter time. My cards were on the mantle piece, Dani was going to St Josephs Catholic School, its not their denomination but Lynne thought the education was of a high standard. We were discussing it and Dani said, just a little boy then, "I don't like RE, learning about Jesus and that." Then he went over to the mantle piece and noticed the picture of Jesus on there. "Oh" he said and quietly went and sat down again. A sign already of a gentle intuitive nature. I said Dani if you think something, say it, no one is going to think less of you.

Not terribly long afterwards he came to visit and he whispered to me, "Joan you know when they all go to the Priest and tell what they've done wrong," "yes" I said, well I go too." he said. Lynne said "well that won't do him any harm will it."

Here I want to tell about another little person who is very dear to me. When we first moved to the lane I was waiting in the bus stop. Another little lady came and sat down beside me, we smiled and began to talk. She was obviously a talker like me and soon we were telling each other things about our lives as if we had always known each other. After that Stan and I would often meet her when we went for our pension. Her name is Linda and little did I know how she would figure in our lives and still does to this day. She lived just up the lane from us but the strangest thing is she was born a few streets away from me, in Redcross Street 15 years after I was born. Her much beloved husband had died quite young and I could see how deeply that had gone with her. I told her about Ludwik to make her feel she was not alone but of course that would never alter the way she felt, everyone is different. She had lived abroad and travelled here, there and everywhere and then after beginning her life a stone throw away from mine, she now lived a few doors away. Fate dictates our lives, sometimes good and sometimes very sadly indeed. But Linda was to become very close to Stan and I. We were like a little band of warriors, Lynne, Linda, Stan and I and later add to that a very caring doctor. They became the nucleus of my life, in fact as time passed they were my life, I clung to them all.

Life went on, by now I was visiting a lady doctor at Neville Road for counselling. I hated waiting for transport to bring me home to Stan, often unravelling the good that had been done. I was now out of Mick's area so I couldn't have him. But that lady doctor probably saved my life in time to come. Before that however, my Stan began to have trouble with is breathing. The doctor gave him something to help him but it got worse. I remember one day watching him fight for breath, he was sitting in the conservatory. I couldn't help him and it was frightening me and breaking my heart to watch. In the early hours of the next morning it got worse and I called an ambulance. They were so kind those men, they put an oxygen mask on him and said it's alright mate you'll be alright now and took him away from me.

I sat for the rest of the night rigid with fear and then I phoned Dorothy, my childhood friend. She came over straight away and stayed with me all day. I phoned our doctor who made enquiries for me at the hospital, my friends and neighbours also phoned and the nurses said to him you must be a VIP to have so many people concerned about you. But he told them it was me they were worried about. I felt as if I was in a fog, so confused. Dorothy had to go home and I was alone. But my doctor phoned about 6pm. "How are you doing" was the comforting question. "Not bad" I said, I was worn out. " think I'll come over "he said. I was never so grateful in my whole life and he came and sat with me for a while. By the time he went I was calmer and feeling I could cope. I had support, oh how I needed it, but for that visit I would have fallen apart.

The next day someone took me up to see him, I was in a fog of fear I can't remember, but almost surely it would have been Lynne. He was all wired up I felt so sad for him, he didn't deserve this, who does though. I blamed myself for all the worry I had given him. Thank god he came home soon, but with so many different tablets! I phoned our doctor as we had been given only a weeks supply. I spelled them out for him and he said that he would send them. After I put the phone down I thought have I told the doctor the right names etc, so I rang Errol at our chemists, he was always a very knowledgeable and helpful person. As I started to spell out the unfamiliar drugs, he was grasping them before I had finished, bless him, what a help he was. Our doctor allowed me a good supply and trusted me with them so that I didn't have to worry. That gentle natured man was my rock through those awful days. I was still attending the doctor at Neville Road and for weeks Stan was in and out of hospital. It was usually at 1am in the morning I had to call the ambulance. Then for a while on the tablets, he settled down. He also had gout, which was very painful. Oh how hard those days were, softened only by Lynne and Linda and the doctors vigilance with us both.

Then one day fate struck again, I started having trouble with my bowels and one day noticed a spot of blood as I got out of bed. I mentioned it to the doctor at Neville Road and she said Joan, I have to inform your doctor about this, I can't let it go, it may be something or nothing but I will write to him. That did it, I thought I'm getting in first here, I didn't want to have to leave my Stan, I was all he had to help him with pills etc, although the doctor was always there if I needed him. So I made an appointment before the letter could reach him and explained to him my dilemma. He examined me, then I dressed and sat with him back in his room. "I'm not leaving him" I said, the doctor obviously thought it a policy not to go into that aspect. He leaned back in his chair and said "we have two options with this, either we give it two weeks to see if it settles down, or you can go up to see a friend of mine at the hospital." I naturally chose the friend, little did I know that was a gentle way to get me there. So an appointment was made. I worried about my Stan but it was obvious there was something wrong with me.

Lynne took me to see the surgeon at the Sussex County Hospital, a very kind man indeed. He said don't make yourself tired explaining your nervous condition, I've had a very informative talk with your GP who has explained the situation. Tears rolled down my cheeks, gentle help again. The surgeon asked me "do you have anyone?" just my husband I replied and he is not in good health and we only have each other. He stood up, came round the desk and embraced me. "We can do things" he said "we can do things." A nightmare was about to begin, my Lynne as ever, was by my side, then and right through the months that were to come, helping me and helping Stan. I was so blessed, most of all with my doctor. I now trusted him as I had never trusted anyone, implicitly. Once again I remembered the visit to Lar in Ashford Road. So began all the tests and I was told I had bowel cancer. I came out and sat staring at the wall. I had come alone that day. It was as if somebody else had been told, not me. Then I thought how am I going to tell Stan, oh god, I'll have to leave him.

I'll never know how he really felt when I told him, he was calm, comforting and reassuring. "We'll manage" he said, "there is always a way." We put our arms around one another and held each other tight as if we could make it all go away. The next step was an ultra sound scan to pin point where the tumour was. I can't remember who went with me, I think this time I went alone. I sat there thinking of going into the tunnel that looked like a big polo mint. The nurse brought me a gigantic jug of something to drink and I didn't know It could take half an hour to do, so I drank it all at once. I felt dizzy, the nurse said "I'm not surprised you didn't have to drink it that quickly, she couldn't help but laugh though. I said "now I shall be wanting to wee." She said "no love, it won't go through it paints your tummy." I think it was iodine. A gentleman in a wheel chair came over to me. "You don't have to be afraid "he said. "I've done it, they won't push you right in." I could have hugged him, with all his own trouble he came to comfort me. I also had a nice young lady sitting with me, because of my nerves, it was arranged that she would meet and stay with me.

So it was time. I was helped on to the trolley bed and they explained what I had to do and said if at any time you want to stop just call out. She said there's a lovely young Irishman working it. I said could you bring him in here, I could do with a lovely young Irishman, she laughed and said that's the spirit. I never asked them to stop, petrified as I was that I'd get stuck in the hole and soon it was over and I felt quite proud because the young nurse said, "Joan, it's people like you who make our work worthwhile, we expected panic, well done." It was over and I could go home. Now I would just have to wait for the date I would have my operation. The surgeon had explained to me that if I wanted him to perform the operation I should have to go to the Princess Royal Hospital in Haywards Heath. I readily agreed, I had taken to him from the first moment of meeting and was not afraid to do as he wished.

I don't remember Christmas that year, our minds were to full of what was to come. My greatest dread was having to leave my beloved husband.

Finally it was arranged for late in January, but I received a phone call from the hospital, the person said "oh Mrs Malek you were to come in on such and such a date", "oh no" I said "please don't say it's been postponed". "Oh no" she said "we want you to come in now." What a relief. The transport was booked, a voluntary driver was to take me over so I packed what I would need and the day dawned when I must leave my Stan. He was quite alright until I was in the car then suddenly he ran down our runway and put his hand in the window. My heart nearly broke, this was worse for him than me. But go I must. I had the preliminary tests and would have the op January 6th 'epiphany'. On the night before the op a very nice man came to talk to me, he would be the one to put me to sleep.

We didn't discuss the op we discussed languages and he told me one could say 'shalom' in Arabic as well as Jewish, a beautiful greeting I always thought. I think it means god be with you, something in that sense. Then he said goodnight, we would meet the next day, my big day. I only had one temazapam tablet for my pre-med, 10ml. So as they wheeled me into the theatre, I said, Shalom, the surgeon glanced around I expect a trifle surprised. The little man I had had such a nice conversation with asked me to sit up on the bed and when he inserted a needle into my lower back, could I please slowly press back into it, I did and I remember no more.

Until in a fuzzy way I heard the surgeon say we have to go back in, in a fuzzy way still I took that to mean something was amiss and was sure. When he said I have to call your husband in Mrs Malek, no! I said emphatically, "please don't he has a bad heart." He tried to explain that he had to but I was adamant. I said "the one up there and you will take care of me tonight, if I'm not here in the morning he will have to know." So it was and I came through the night. I slowly surfaced in intensive care. A very kind team were wiping my mouth and watching over me. They gave me little sticks with moist sponges on them to touch my lips with. I said can I suck them I am so thirsty, yes she said and I called them lollipops. A young man standing near heard me say may I have another lollipop, "what does she mean," he asked. He probably thought I was out of it but the nurse explained.

A week later back in a normal ward a young man approached my bed and I asked him "are you the man from the church?" "No lollipop" he replied. " I've come from intensive care to see how you are." The staff in that hospital were absolutely wonderful and the care I received the same. The next thing I had to come to terms with was that part of my anatomy was outside my body and had to be attended to by a colostomy bag. I also had a chest infection but funnily enough I wasn't afraid, only worried about my Stan. One day, a lady receptionist came in to the ward and said who is the VIP here, Mrs Malek. She said my GP had phoned to say my Stan was alright and sent his love. How nice can things be, I cried with relief and gratitude. One human can sometimes help another human in such a wonderful way, I never forgot that call, or forgot how lucky I was to have people that cared.

Soon I was trying to help myself and the stoma nurse was very pleased with me. But trouble was looming, I suddenly felt ill and I developed an abscess not far from the stoma. I had seen a lot of activity and cleaning etc going on. One day after a violent reaction to Imodium, (my body is really sensitive to all sorts of things) the doctor decided to lance and clean the abscess under local anaesthetic. Little did he know I had MRSA, the dreaded enemy stalking the hospitals. My doctor had requested I was not be told because of my nervous state, how grateful I am that he did. But I asked the Sister to phone Stan and tell him not to visit for a bit, it was obvious there was some infection and I couldn't risk that.

Eventually I was allowed to go home, I still couldn't change myself for fear of infecting my wound from the abscess. When I got home at 5pm, I phoned the surgery straight away as advised and by 7pm the nurses were already there. I couldn't go up the stairs and my husband had to do so much for me. He nursed me so lovingly, cooked me nice meals etc. I worried for him but through our mutual suffering we were growing so close to each other, we had constant care from our doctor and help from Lynne and Linda. It was a bittersweet comradeship but in it's way very beautiful, deep and it brought out the best in us.

After six months I went back in for the reversal, came home on my birthday, June 8th, but was rushed back the next morning, they feared there was a blockage. But after ten days I came home again. Thank god we were on our way up, no more changing bags etc and the doctor kept an eye on us and good thing too. For my final trick I developed ulcers in some part of where I'd had the op. the doctor said "I think you will have to have another endoscopy" but at first I said no. The doctor said "I can't make you but I think you should." About an hour later I thought it over and then phoned him and said you are right doctor, I'll do whatever you want.

Out of that came the scare that I might have cancer in another part of my tummy but the biopsies proved not. I waited for two weeks to find out and then went to see my surgeon for the results. They were good and he phoned my doctor while I was there and I had to take the pills the size of bombs to cure the ulcers, in fact they were so large I didn't know exactly how to use them, when I phoned the young lady laughed and said "you take them by mouth Joan."

So slowly we pulled out of it all, like a slow heavy train puffing along. Stan was taking a lot of pills still but we were still together, our friends still looking after us. We shared the jobs, Stan would hoover, I would dust and phone through our orders for food, it was delivered. Stan cooked and I washed up and our doctor phoned frequently to see how we were managing, those phone calls kept me going and gave me courage. The district nurses were still calling and so our life moved on. Lynne was constantly with us, she cut our hair and gave me heart to carry on.

So we lived our lives as best we could. Linda popped in often and we, all three would sit and chat. I never was without the fear that lived with me, I was given numbers to ring if I felt that I couldn't cope. Everyone was so kind. My Lynne used to come and see us regularly.

Nights were the worst, I never really slept deeply. It was like having a child to look after. The doctor called frequently and I would get Stan ready to save him time. I realise now what a pressure it put on him but he only ever showed kind patience.

At night if I thought I smelled the spray Stan used to help him I would get up and go into him. If he was sitting up, I'd know I had to call an ambulance, he struggled for breath and it broke my heart. Then the doctor assigned a matron from the community nurses for Stan, I thought for me as well. Ignorance is bliss. Gradually things got worse. On Saturday morning my doctor called in and couldn't resist checking him he said and as he left, "you do know he is a very poorly man don't you." I did, I had been hiding it from myself. I said to the doctor "it's like a woman near to giving birth, scrubs the house down and prepares." My Stan is preparing, I can't remember if my doctor answered. It must be so hard for them and so often. He said goodbye and I looked round the door at three little faces peeping out of the car, his children. I went into Janet and I said Jan, I'm watching my husband die. She said "oh don't say that," but now I knew and so did he.

I realise now he was checking his own slowing pulse with the watch I still have and kiss because it was close to him. I heard him say to members of his family one day, "I don't know how long I've got." My heart was breaking, I would put my arms around him and hold him close so that one day I would be able to remember the way it felt. Then I can't remember how came the Sunday when we had three nurses with us. Stan was very bad by then. Suddenly he asked if he could have some more of his medicine, morphine, I think, and then he turned to me and said "no matter where I'll be, I'll always love you". One of the nurses was very touched.

They decided it was time to call the doctor who unbeknown to me was expecting it. This was not to happen at home I learned he had said. The nurse said to me, Joan, do you know what the doctor was doing? Gardening, I thought how lovely he is putting life in the ground and my Stan's is ebbing away. It was like a circle closing. I felt a little better. We waited quite a long time, agony, then the ambulance came, my poor darling Stan apologised because he couldn't stand up. Oh how it hurt me to see this. The ambulance man was so gentle and kind, "never mind mate" he said, "were here to help you." And so my boy went out of our house for the last time, feeling I know so very bad, I was numb with misery. I said to the nurses "he's not coming back this time is he?" And she kindly answered "you never know." But he was going to the Martlets, gateway to heaven.

I sat with the nurses for a while and then they left and I was alone. They left all kinds of numbers to ring but what would that avail me now. I phoned my Lynne, she loved my

Stan also. Darran answered and as fate would have it Lynne wasn't far from the Martlets, Dani was playing football out there and she went to Stan. She said he was so pleased to see her but she said to me, Joan, I think we had better go to see him tomorrow. So we did. Oh god he looked so ill, but he looked across at Lynne and she said "they are in the fridge," he turned to me and said "they let me have grapes in here." I broke up inside, I had had to be so careful about his gout and he did so want sharp acidy things, how does one decide. Then he kind of slept and I kept telling him in Polish, "I love you, do you hear. I love you." And then we left him to rest. That was our goodbye, goodbye to my darling Staszek who had said when we met, "you I remember", now I would have only memories.

At 1am the next morning I was awoken by a ring at the bell. I went down and Lynne said "its me." I thought I was wanted at the hospital. Lynne was in her nightie and slippers. I couldn't tell you this over the phone she said, "Stan passed away not long ago." I stood in my nightie an cried out over and over, "oh no, god no." Lynne sat quietly on the stairs, it must have distressed her badly but she stayed the night on the couch and me in the armchair.

Dawn crept into the sky, my beloved had gone, his spirit like a dove had flown free, god rest him.

Suddenly I was calm, there was a lot we had to do for him, for his family, a lot to arrange. My Lynne was my rock, I can't remember if I called the doctor, everything was a mist I was trying to see through.

Somehow it all got done. Polish funeral arranged with Mrs Zawada, I had not met as yet. Father Tadeus, postponed his holiday so as to preside over it. Mrs Zawada who became my very dear friend arranged the reception for afterwards.

The funeral was arranged for the 7th of July. Francois and Joycelyne were going to come and Lynne said she would bring some refreshments for them for when they arrived. They arrived and Jean Claude came with them. Little Linda came down and waited with us. When Lynne arrived with the food she looked so beautiful in a chic but tasteful dress, I saw Francois glance at her, a Frenchman's eye for beauty. I didn't know how I felt, just a steady knowledge of what was going on. Time passed and it was time for Stan to come to his home for the last time, we drove slowly up the lane, nothing felt real.

The mass was beautiful with Father Tadeus presiding. My white heart with red roses rested on his coffin, he was taking my heart with him. Stella Posiadla was there and Terry, Marcel's sister-in-law, also the lovely little matron who had taken care of Stan. She smiled as I passed her on the way out from the church. She told me afterwards, Joan I didn't understand a word but it was one of the most dignified funerals I have ever been to. I had given him back to his people, perhaps now his soul had gone home. At the service in the crematorium, Father Tadeus was all in white. I held up alright until the final curtains closed and then my heart was breaking.

We drove to the Polish club and the tables looked lovely, but we had a mishap, Francois and the others had somehow got lost behind a traffic light perhaps, and I had to go back home to check if they had gone back home to my house , but no. Later on I phoned Francois and Simon told me that they had got lost and were on their way home. Ursula had packed food up for me to take home and I gave it to Ella and her husband to take back to London. They had to go and then I was alone, lost in the darkness of loss. Somehow I got into bed and slept.

Lynne made an appointment for us to go and see Stan at the chapel and although she really didn't want to, she took some photos of him for me to send to Poland, as is the custom. Poor Lynne she had not long lost her own mother, but she was brave for my sake and I was so grateful. I could close the book on all I could do for the family.

The next day my doctor came to see me and he said "he looked very peaceful". Right to the end that gentle doctor helped me survive. How I got through the next weeks I really don't know. I wandered the house and sat in the kitchen that he had struggled to paint for me and I sobbed until I couldn't stand. My Lynne came often she was fostering a little baby called Jack. He seemed to have been sent to both of us, we were both suffering loss. Linda came in quite often, but I only wanted Stan.

The chapter of our life together was over, no more checking if my man was alright, just an awful silence. I used to sit on the steps and watch the traffic going by, thinking of the passengers, you don't know how the girl on the steps is aching, so unbearably. The little kind matron no longer came, everyone seemed to be melting into the past. I had a few numbers I could call but when one puts the phone down the silence is worse.

So the days passed on, leaden wings, finally, I thought I'm going to sell the house and go into a home. I picked up the phone book and the first home I saw was the Princess Alexandra. I rang and the owner asked me would you like me to pick you up now? Within half an hour I had looked at the home, paid a deposit on a room and returned home to put the house on the market. Then began a hard few months, oh so very hard to do it by myself.

I had a prospective buyer but that turned out not to be suitable and I rang the agents and said call it off please I can't afford to keep dilly dallying and bringing down the price. I put the phone down and panicked. Lynne and Darran were in Barbados on holiday so I rang Lynne's sister, Shirley. She was so kind she said put the phone down Joan but stay by it for about ten minutes, which I did. Suddenly it rang and it was Darran, he said if it was still going at the same price he would buy it and he would ring his Solicitor and begin negotiations and that's just what he did. But long before all this Lynne and I had laid Stan to rest. I chose a spot for his ashes right near where my parents had theirs, by the side of a little waterfall, just the other side of a tiny bridge that spanned the water. A place where there would be perfect peace but for the sound of the water and birds, where butterflies and dragonflies would hover in the summer. The rose tree would be for us both, so one day I would be there. Lynne and I went up one day to place the urn in the earth, I couldn't bend or hold the urn for long, it was quite heavy put beautiful. The lady from the office fetched the gardener who prepared his resting place and my Lynne and I stood there, as always together. She had on a pure white sort of Muslim trouser suit and I remember thinking, she looks like an angel. The lady asked me do you want a service but I said no I will do it. So I said the hail Mary in English and in Polish and Lynne and I walked away. She held my hand and I never loved her more. She took me up to the restaurant at the Racehill and we ate together. It was done, the roses would bloom, the breeze would blow upon them and there was perfect peace all around. I could do no more for my man. From now on it was a journey without him but I had my Lynne, also Linda and my doctor still came a few times more and phoned. When it came time for that to stop it really hurt. One forgets there are other patients and I now had to step back into the ranks which didn't mean in anyway that the care I had would not be there if I needed it.

Now it was crunch time. My home would be Darrans, which I was happy about. No stranger would have it and I had to think about getting into the Princess Alexandra. Christmas was coming up and I received a letter from Carole, who owned the home saying if I would be alone, I would be welcome to go there and that she would come to fetch me and bring me home. I accepted, Christmas alone at home, no one next door, I couldn't face it. I didn't even know how I could bear it without Stan. So many years our little tree had stood and we had spent a quiet but happy time together. So it was arranged, Christmas in the home was done quite beautifully, what I call a Dickens one. The staff were all very kind and to top it all Carole said "I have a surprise for you" and took me into a lovely room with a balcony overlooking Preston Park. I paid the extra deposit straight away, the room was made for me.

The other residents were very nice, one in particular, a Dutch lady whose name was Jenny. She was so kind and thoughtful to me. Her life had been very hard, she had lived in Holland under Nazi occupation and suffered dreadfully. She kept encouraging me, she said "I've had 20 years like this, you learn to deal with it." So, my first Christmas without Stan. Carole took me back home on Boxing night, my wedding anniversary, it still hurts to remember the silence.

Then came New Years Eve, everyone was away, I was alone in the lane and I got into such a state, I phoned my surgery and a little later a very nice young doctor phoned, I talked with him and slowly I felt better. But it felt like I would never heal.

My own doctor said he knew the home and couldn't wait to

get me in there. A caring doctor needs to know his patients are safe, but life was changing, the surgery was becoming very busy, rules were changed, beaurocracy was growing. I could feel times were changing and it seemed to me the world shifted under my feet. All I had clung to was still there but time moves on, even if I couldn't.

Darran had said if I needed any money (the house was still under Probate) he would help me and the outcome was he gave me an advance on the house and I was able to go into the home. I left everything just as it was and left. Some things went to the Martlets charities, some I think to Emaeus, I didn't really care, I just didn't want to be alone anymore. On the second day I was in there, my doctor called, I was so grateful it made things less strange for me and not such a clean break of all I had known. But I sensed that now things would be different, I was in care and I felt cold inside and lonely as if something would never be the same again.

Jenny and I became close friends, she introduced me to her friends who invited me out to art exhibitions and to tea. Also we had a musician come every so often and I would actually dance, yes dance.

I loved watching the sun rise and set from my balcony, it was so beautiful. In that park I overlooked, I had played as a child, done my courting, walked with my two husbands and friends. I sat in the garden and dreamed and remembered. I knitted countless garments for folk there, also Age Concern. I was happy there for while, the only drawback was it wasn't quite warm enough in my room, it was large and under the roof and I couldn't make them understand my dilemma. When the heating was turned down at ground level, I heard mine click off completely and in the end my nerves were suffering and after three years there I decided to leave.

Lynne took me to see another place as I was in a rush, I decided and in we moved. It was not quite what I wanted and to make matters worse on the third day I was there, I received news from Canada that my sister, Edna, had died. I was absolutely stricken. The owners were very kind and comforting but I needed my doctor. I rang but he wasn't there, another doctor was very gentle and kind. I didn't settle down however until my own doctor rang, somehow I always responded to him, I was comforted, but oh the less.

After about six weeks I knew I had to move again. Poor Lynne, what she had to put up with me. However she and Shirley helped me once again. Here I must pause in my story to see how things will pan out.

Things have panned out and now I am safely ensconced in my Lynne's home, in my own room which will now be my haven. So we can continue.

I have left my third and last rest home. Whilst everyone was kind, I was very lonely and every time Lynne left it was getting worse. I have grown very low and must now pick up again. Thoughts come to haunt, I still don't like long periods on my own, I have pain in my left hand which is impeding my knitting etc. I must make an effort to come up again for my Lynne's sake, my every comfort has been taken care of. Lynne's gone like a whirlwind through my wardrobe and everything has been washed and has its place, a clean start.

Now when I look back on my last move into the last rest home I shiver.

The ground was covered with ice, Lynne and Shirley had a dreadful job carrying suitcases etc, a nightmare. I was still deeply grieving over my sister, cold outwards and inside.

Somehow we managed. They had to put towels down over the ice to get me out of one place and into another. Then came the trauma of yet another strange room and system, the residents were very nice and the staff but my heart ached when Lynne and Shirley left. Christmas came and went and I could feel nothing, I felt like lead inside.

Then after a week or so my doctor came for a visit. My spirits lifted a little but it was of no avail, when he went, I sat in the chair in the corner of my room, so, so sad and dejected. It looked out over a courtyard and a pond which for some reason made me feel even sadder.

One day while my friend Marian was visiting the phone rang, that was to change my life yet again. Lynne said she and the family had agreed that it would be better if I went to live with her. My heart beat faster and faster, it sounds like heaven I said.

So we had a chairlift put in which I thought was great of Lynne to have such a thing in her 'young' home and then I sat back to await the great day.

So here I am. The view from the back of the house looks right out over the downs, its beautiful. Also I am conscious that I am not far from my Ludwik and Stan's resting place. Somehow that comforts. I thought Linda might find me a visit today but it hasn't happened. So things must change yet again.

Last night, Chris, Jade's partner put rails down the steps to Lynne's hairdressing salon. I had my hair washed and incidentally, my clothes, so have had to change, I must get used to the backward wash. But everyone has bent over backwards to help me and I really must try. I sit here and write and Jerry the cat sits on my bed, his mate, Tom, is somewhere about.

So life goes on since Stan died I have been tossed about like a cork on the ocean but am hoping for a fairly calm sea now. The family have many things in mind for me, I'm trying so hard to rid myself of the sadness that threatens like a tidal wave to overwhelm me, any emotion can make me unstable.

Today I have been sad, Lynne went away for a couple of days, Shirley has looked after me fine but I have a sadness inside that will not pass away. From the window up here one can see the lights of the town and for some reason that tugged at my heart. Beauty without the beloved is a sword through the heart. I sit here alone in my room and look at a photograph of Edna, Stan and myself in happier times and I long to be with them. The family don't like me to feel that way and speak of lovely things we will do together. But today, Good Friday, my emotions crucified me. I hope I can be brave and reward their kindness, my future is in good hands.

So there I will let the present rest. In case my story seems to be a catalogue of sorrows, there have been many rapturous times, beautiful moments. A wonderful childhood, magical due to my mothers enthusiasm to make it so, all the interesting jobs I have done in my life, the wonderful friends who have entered and left my life. My introduction to the Polish life and culture which began with the war and has lasted all my life. The beauty of Poland comes to me through the nostalgic music of Chopin and the poet Slowacski. The history so sad but always head up and brave. I would wish to be that brave but somehow it escapes me, my heart can break so very easily, the sadness that comes is so painful. But good happy times were there. It's Easter and on Easter Saturday, 1948 I was baptised into the Catholic church by Father Walsh, who really gave me a soaking. My faith to this day is my joy,

I made my first communion on Easter Sunday. I will never forget the beauty of that, the taking away of the purple covers and everything becoming golden. The Priests Glory ringing through the church and the sound of joyous hand bells shaken by altar boys. Everything was still in Latin then and I loved it. I knelt for my first communion with Ludwik with great joy. This Easter there is pain of loss inside me but I must try to live up to the kindness of my Lynne and her family. I don't want to leave her my hurt. Maybe, just maybe, there will be readers of my humble saga and I hope they will get to know me through it and maybe say a prayer, for that I need.

A long journey, now with the loneliness of the long distance runner, but we are born into families like flowers in a garden. We bloom and one by one our special little garden fades, to be the last bloom is hard, but now I'm in another family garden. Not far from here bloom the roses of Stan's resting place and the eagle stands over Ludwik's photo at the foot of his cross and one day when the essence of my life is beneath those roses, I hope my beloved Lynne will come and be not sad but remember our journey together with all it has held and our angels will be with her.

I want to end with the words from a Polish poem written on Stan's memorial plaque by Juliasz Stowack.

They are so... Ah, even the happiest of men does not know where the spirits fold their wings nor where they sit like swans a dream.

THE END

Lightning Source UK Ltd.
Milton Keynes UK
UKHW01f0619210618
324580UK00001B/130/P